BOWLERS, BROLLIES, AND BRITS

CURIOUS HISTORIES OF ENGLAND

MARGO LESTZ

BOO-TICKETY PUBLISHING

ISBNs:

Paperback: 978-1-8380933-0-3
E-pub: 978-1-8380933-1-0
Mobi: 978-1-8380933-2-7

CONTENTS

INTRODUCTION

BEFORE WE BEGIN...

Hello and welcome to *Bowlers, Brollies, and Brits.*

I'm American by birth and some stories in this book were inspired by things that were unfamiliar to me when I first moved to England. But most of them are just a result of my curiosity. England is an old country, full of stories and legends. And I love it. Nothing thrills me more than discovering some little-known bit of history—the quirkier the better. I call these stories my *curious histories* and I share them on my blog and in my books.

This book is a collection of stories that I've gathered over the years which are related in some way or another to England and the English. It's not meant to be a comprehensive volume on the entire country, but a light, often humorous, selection of stories and histories that I found interesting. I hope you'll like them too.

Happy reading!

WHERE AM I?

UNITED KINGDOM? GREAT BRITAIN?
ENGLAND? BRITISH ISLES?

*T*here are so many different terms related to this area that I thought we should just sort them all out at the beginning. The stories in this book are mostly about England, but you'll notice that sometimes I use Britain, Great Britain, and the UK as well.

I live in the country of England, but I have a UK passport. I also live in Great Britain and the British Isles. And no, I don't have four different homes—one place can actually be called by all these names.

Let's see if we can unravel this twisting trail of terms:

GREAT BRITAIN

Great Britain is a landmass surrounded by water—in other words, it's an island. Three independent countries (England, Scotland, and Wales) are situated on the island of Great Britain.

UNITED KINGDOM

Add the country of Northern Ireland into the above mix, and you get the United Kingdom of Great Britain and Northern Ireland. This rather lengthy title is usually shortened to the United Kingdom or the UK.

BRITISH ISLANDS

Tack on the Isle of Man, Guernsey, and Jersey—three islands which are self-governing crown dependencies—and you will have the British Islands (not to be confused with the British Isles).

BRITISH ISLES

Add in the State of Ireland and lots of tiny islands and you have the British Isles. However, this term is controversial and to be avoided—especially in Ireland.

This little chart might help to keep it all straight.

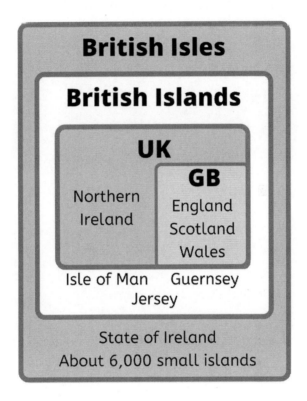

So now, when anyone asks me where I'm from, I can confidently answer: "I'm from England... which is on the island of Great Britain... which is part of the United Kingdom... which is part of the British Islands... which is part of the British Isles..."

Or maybe I'll just say, "I'm from London."

I

BRITISH STEREOTYPE

WHAT DOES AN ENGLISHMAN WEAR?

Bowlers
and
Brollies

BOWLERS, CITY GENTS, AND STEREOTYPES

WHAT DOES THE HAT HAVE TO DO WITH IT?

*I*sn't it funny how hats are used in national stereotypes? If you see a cartoon of a man in a beret, you immediately know he's supposed to be French. A cowboy hat means he's American, and a bowler says he's British.

The British bowler has a long and interesting history. Originally it sat atop English gamekeepers' heads, then the heads of all social classes. Later it became the trademark of the City Gentleman and the basis for the British stereotype that's still recognizable today.

From the 1940s through the 1970s, the streets of London's financial district were teeming with City Gents. The City Gent wore a dark suit and carried an umbrella which doubled as a walking stick, but the most distinguishing part of his ensemble had to be his neat and practical little bowler hat.

HISTORY OF THE BOWLER

The humble British bowler's story begins in 1849 on Lord Coke's large estate in Norfolk, England. Like most of the nobility of his day, Lord Coke's favorite pastimes were hunting and fishing. He employed lots of gamekeepers to take care of his land and to make sure there was always game ready for his sporting pleasure. Sometimes they also had to chase off poachers who were looking for their dinner on Coke's land.

The gamekeepers on such an important estate had to look their best, and that meant they were required to wear top hats—the tall gentlemanly hat of the day. However, those high hats were hard to keep on. Every time a gamekeeper would duck into some underbrush, ride beneath a low-hanging branch, or even gallop after a poacher, their top hat would topple to the ground and be trampled by their horse. Even after they secured them to the collars of their coats with cords, they were still getting dented and damaged. The hats were simply too delicate for the rough life of a gamekeeper.

A NEW AND PRACTICAL HAT

One day, when yet another hat had been ruined, Lord Coke decided enough was enough. He made a trip to London and went to Lock & Co. Hatters on St. James's Street. They had a reputation for making hats to special requirements, so Lord Coke described his ideal gamekeeper's hat to them: "It should be close-fitting and snug so it won't be knocked off by branches and won't fly off in the wind. In addition, it should be sturdy so that if a horse steps on it, it will hold its shape. And, lastly, it should protect the gamekeeper's head from blows, either accidental or by poacher attacks."

Lock & Co. assured Lord Coke they would come up with something acceptable. Then they passed the specifications on to their most talented hat maker, Thomas Bowler, who worked up a prototype. He designed a felt hat with a small brim and a low melon-shaped dome. Then he injected the felt with a special, secret-recipe stiffener which basically turned the hat into a hard helmet.

HOW TO TEST A NEW HAT

In December 1849 Lord Coke came back to see what they had come up with. He took the hat in his hands and turned it all around for a good look. He tapped on it with his knuckles, then he threw it down on the floor and stomped on it. The hat showed no dents, so he stomped on it again even harder. Still, it held its original shape. Lord Coke was satisfied with the new design and ordered them for all his gamekeepers.

As was the practice with custom-made hats, it was named after the client who ordered it. So this one became the coke hat or the Billycock (Billy Coke). But as it gained popularity, it took the name of its designer, Thomas Bowler, and became the bowler hat.

SUCCESS STORY

The bowler was originally designed for gamekeepers, but soon all types of workmen discovered its practicality. Laborers everywhere needed a hat that would stay put, protect the head, and wouldn't get in the way. It was the first hard hat, and it was adopted by shipyard workers, train drivers, street traders, bus drivers, etc. Train drivers are said to have tested their hats by sticking their heads out of a fast-moving train. If it didn't blow off, it was a good fit.

THE HAT FOR EVERYMAN

This practical little hat even managed to cross the lines of the British class system. In the 1860s Prince Albert Edward (Queen Victoria's son, who would become King Edward VII) was seen wearing a bowler. It became an acceptable gentleman's hat and was especially popular with bankers and civil servants. Even while these City Gents were wearing bowlers to their banking jobs, men from the lower classes were still wearing them while selling carrots or working on the trains. The bowler was truly a hat for everyman.

DECLINE OF THE BOWLER

After the Second World War, lots of things changed, and lower-class men began to go hatless. The City Gents in their bowlers were almost the only remaining hat wearers until this fashion also began to fade in the 1970s.

Even though bowlers are rarely seen on the streets today, they live on in our memories. Who can forget Charlie Chaplin's Little Tramp waddling along in his bowler? Chaplin, along with Laurel and Hardy, used the bowler as a prop in their comedy routines. And Mr. Banks from Mary Poppins is the perfect cliché of a City Gent with his suit, bowler, and brolly going off to work at the bank.

NOT COMPLETELY GONE

The bowler hasn't completely disappeared from modern British life. It's not a hat that you'll see very often, but it's still worn in certain sectors. Bowlers and closed brollies are the uniform for retired cavalrymen to wear when on parade, and female police officers have the option of wearing a bowler. On the Holkham Hall estate, where the idea for the bowler was born, the gamekeepers still proudly sport them. But they must be earned: Only after completing one year of good service, is a gamekeeper awarded his own bowler from Lock & Co.

USA

The bowler hat was a good design, and like most good ideas, it spread. It traveled to America, where it was first associated with horse races. The races were called derbies after the Earl of Derby who organized the Epsom Downs horse race in the UK. Therefore, in the US, the bowler hat took the name derby. And from the horse races, the bowler (or derby) made its way to the West where it was popular with cowboys and outlaws such as Butch Cassidy and the Sundance Kid.

BOLIVIA

It's not terribly surprising that a British hat traveled to America, but Bolivia? The bowler migrated to the South American country in the 1920s when the British were building railroads there. As the story goes, a shipment of bowler hats arrived from England for the British railway workers. But there was a mix-up and all the hats were too small to fit the men.

So some clever marketing person decided to sell them to Bolivian women and tout them as the latest European fashion. The group of women who adopted the bowler as their own later came to be known as Cholas. They were rural women recently arrived in the city, and they loved the hat so much that they made it part of their traditional dress. They wear it sitting high on top of the head and the way it's worn can indicate marital status. Over the years, the style has been altered slightly and the hats are now manufactured locally.

LOCK & CO.

The unassuming bowler has had an amazing history sitting atop the heads of British gamekeepers, bankers, kings, and carrot sellers, as well as American outlaws and Bolivian Cholas. And it all began at Lock & Co. in London. They've been making hats at No. 6 St. James's Street since 1765 and are still going strong. So, if you're in London and in the market for a very special hat, you can probably find it there. They sell head coverings of all descriptions—including the very British bowler.

JONAS HANWAY
CARRIED AN UMBRELLA

THE BRITISH BROLLY'S FIRST ADVOCATE

The umbrella (or brolly) is an integral part of the British stereotype for obvious reasons: It rains a lot in the UK. So, you would think that the Brits would have adopted the brolly as soon as it was invented. But they didn't. Not until Jonas Hanway paved the way.

Jonas was born in Portsmouth, on the south coast of England, and his travels began at age seventeen when he was apprenticed to a merchant in Lisbon, Portugal. Later he returned to London and set up his own business. Things began to get interesting, though, in 1743 when, at age thirty-one, he partnered with a textile trader in St. Petersburg, Russia. He set out from Russia to Persia (now Iran) on a mission to form new trade alliances. He succeeded, but only after a year and a half filled with many harrowing experiences.

When he returned to England in 1750 at age thirty-eight, he became very civic-minded and got involved in all sorts of social issues: He founded the Marine Society to recruit and train seamen, was vice president of a children's home, established a home for "fallen women," worked toward getting streets paved, and campaigned against using little boys as chimney sweeps. For some reason, he was also against tea drinking, and naturalizing Jews. He wrote profusely and published many pamphlets. But what is Jonas Hanway most remembered for...? He carried an umbrella.

JONAS CARRIED AN UMBRELLA

Yes, Jonas Hanway was the first man in England to carry a brolly. Umbrellas were nothing new, they had been used in various forms around the world since ancient times. But they were mostly parasols used in hot countries to keep off the sun. Then in the seventeenth century, the French began coating parasols with wax to keep off the rain. They also developed the folding umbrella as we know it today. Even though French brollies were used by both sexes, in England, they were considered a strictly feminine article. Real men either got wet or took a taxi.

So when Jonas was seen in the streets of London with his brolly, some laughed at him, some called him effeminate, or worse—a Frenchie. And the cabbies were really upset. Seeing a man on the street with an umbrella meant that he wouldn't be hailing a cab and they didn't want that to catch on. They threw taunts, jeers, and even rotten fruit at him.

But did that bother Jonas? Not a bit. You see, when he was in Persia on his first overseas trading trip, he had experienced much worse...

WARS COULDN'T STOP HIM

He arrived in Persia with a load of English cloth that he planned to trade for silk. But almost as soon he arrived, he was caught up in a regional uprising and was captured in Astrabad. All his cloth was stolen, and he was almost taken as a slave before he managed to escape. He traveled for nearly a month (250 miles) on foot, horseback, camel, and leaky boat, all the while dodging the roaming rebel forces. He was going to find the Shah and ask to be reimbursed for his losses.

Jonas finally found the Shah, who was preparing for a battle against the rebels. After the Shah had made him wait a few days, Jonas was allowed to present his request. The Shah said, "OK, no problem. I'll reimburse you for what the rebels stole. Just take this note back to my general in Astrabad and he'll sort it out for you."

DO IT ALL AGAIN

Astrabad! Jonas gritted his teeth and began the perilous 250-mile journey back to where he had just come from. The Shah dispatched a few guards to accompany him, but they soon disappeared, and he was left on his own. On the way back, poor Jonas faced all the same perils as before with the addition of being stalked by hungry wolves.

After a month and a half, he arrived back in Astrabad and showed the letter to the general who said, "Ok, no problem. We'll sort it out, but it'll take a few days." After a few weeks had passed, Jonas went back to the general to ask about his money. The general admitted that the Shah had taken some of it, so he could only give Jonas about 85%. But he offered to give him some slave girls whom he could sell to make up the difference. Jonas politely declined the slaves and left with his 85%.

I WANT MY SILK

But Jonas wasn't about to give up and go home yet. No, he was going to get his silk. After all, that's why he had come. So he set off on a 180-mile journey to Reshd. He arrived in September 1744—a year after he had landed in Persia. He was finally within reach of the silk he had come for. Unfortunately, due to the rough year he had had, he became very ill and took two months to recover. But as soon as he was well, he bought his silk and jumped on a ship back to Russia.

After a little run-in with pirates, the ship reached the shores of Russia. But the authorities said that plague had been reported in Persia, and he would have to be quarantined for six weeks. Finally, nearly a year and a half after he had set out on his journey, Jonas returned to St. Petersburg silk in hand. He had gone for silk and, by golly, he had brought it back.

PERSIAN WARRIORS OR LONDON CABBIES?

So when the London cabbies called Jonas names and threw things at him, he hardly even noticed. He completely ignored them and just went about his business—in the rain with his perfectly practical umbrella keeping him dry. And as it turned out, his brolly also made a good shield when rotten fruit was thrown at him.

Eventually, as other soaking wet English men saw him walking along nice and dry under his umbrella, they decided it wasn't such a bad idea after all. Today nearly every self-respecting Londoner carries a brolly. And it's all thanks to the brave and determined Jonas Hanway.

- If you are in London and would like to see a Victorian brolly shop, go to James Smith & Sons, 53 New Oxford Street, London WC1A 1BL The shop has remained practically unchanged since 1857 when it moved to these premises. They also have a portrait of Jonas Hanway in their shop to honor the man who started it all.

II

FOOD AND DRINK

YOU'VE GOT TO EAT!

Tea
Fish and Chips
and More

A PROPER CUP OF TEA
AND HOW IT ALL BEGAN

*W*here would the British be without their tea? Even though they've lovingly adopted the brown beverage, the tea plant is not native to their island. So let's have a look at where tea came from and how people started drinking it in the first place. Then later we'll find out how to make the perfect cuppa.

IT ALL STARTED IN CHINA

Legend says that the first cup of tea was brewed in China around 2500 BC quite by accident. Shen Nung, who is considered the father of Chinese medicine, was traveling through the country snacking on plants to find out which ones were poisonous and then trying to find antidotes for them. He was said to have had a transparent body which made it easier for him to see the plant's effects.

One afternoon, Shen Nung stopped for what turned out to be the world's first tea break. He built a fire and put a pot of water on to boil—being a scientific man, he knew that boiled water was safer to drink. He gathered some dried branches of the nearby *Camellia sinensis* (tea plant) to make his fire. As the wood burned, the wind carried some of the dried leaves into the air and they fell into his boiling water. The result: the very first brew of tea. Of course, the curious Shen Nung had a sip of the colored liquid. Not only did he find the taste pleasing, but he was convinced it would work as an antidote to some of the poisonous herbs that he planned to sample later on. After some experimentation, he concluded that he could counteract the toxic effects of around seventy plants with a cup of tea.

Unfortunately, for Shen Nung, one poisonous plant proved fatal. Its toxins worked so quickly that he didn't even have time to drink his tea antidote before his intestines exploded.

Today, most of us don't wander through the woods nibbling on poisonous plants, but we still drink tea—just because we like it.

HOW TO MAKE A PROPER CUPPA

Shen Nung enjoyed his tea made with just the basics: a pot of boiling water and dried tea leaves. And that's really all that's necessary. But some of us modern folk are a bit more finicky about how we brew our cuppa. After 4,500 years of tea consumption, making a proper cup of tea has turned into an art.

So, how do you make the perfect cup of tea? There are probably just about as many answers to that question as there are tea drinkers. Everyone has their preference for a certain tea blend, serving temperature, sweetness, milkiness, etc. Whatever suits you is your perfect cup of tea. However, there are a few recommendations to help you brew your perfect cuppa:

- Fill the kettle with fresh, cold water. Oxygen in water helps the flavor develop, so don't be tempted to reheat any previously boiled water.
- After the water comes to a boil, give it a few minutes to cool down. Pouring boiling water over tea leaves will burn them and keep them from releasing their full flavor. After the water has rested two or three minutes, pour it over the tea.
- Let the tea leaves steep. Different kinds of teas have different brewing times which are usually noted on the packet. Of course, it's up to you to decide how much time is just right.
- After the tea leaves have steeped, remove them from the water. Over-brewing will make a bitter beverage.

Whether you make your tea in a pot or directly in the cup, these tips will help you make a flavorful cup of tea. Be sure to use your favorite mug or cup for added enjoyment. Bone china or porcelain are normally recommended for best results.

ARE YOU A MIFFY OR A TIFFY?

A controversy has long raged about whether milk should be added to the cup before the tea or after. There are two camps: The Miffys (milk in first) and the Tiffys (tea in first). This debate, like most things, has its roots in history.

In the early days of tea-drinking in the UK, cups were not of the quality they are today, and pouring hot water into them could cause them to crack. So, everyone was a Miffy and poured their milk into the cup first to cool the tea a bit and keep the cup intact.

When fine china arrived in Britain, the upper crust became Tiffys and took to putting their tea in first. This had nothing to do with flavor: It was just to show everyone that they owned the best quality china and it was strong enough (and expensive enough) to take the heat.

If you are feeling pretty comfortable with your social standing, then feel free to add milk to your tea whenever you feel like it. You can even bypass the milk altogether, it's entirely up to you. With that said, however, here are a few milk considerations:

- Tea brews best in hot water. That means that if you are steeping the tea in a cup, it's probably better to add the milk after the tea has steeped. If using a pot, the tea has already brewed, so it doesn't matter which goes into your cup first.
- Putting milk in first then adding your already-brewed tea results in a creamier tea and cools it to a more drinkable temperature.

Now, go put the kettle on and brew yourself the perfect cuppa!

- In London, the oldest tea shop is Twinings at 216 Strand, WC2R 1AP. Tea has been sold in this narrow little shop for more than 300 years.

TEA — AFTERNOON TEA — HIGH TEA
WHAT'S THE DIFFERENCE?

*T*he English love their tea, but just what is tea? It seems that little word can have several meanings. Everyone knows tea is a beverage, but the word tea might also refer to a meal: It could be a snack or light meal around 4:00 pm which is called afternoon tea, or tea can be another name for dinner. Both of these very different meals might simply be called "tea". Let's see if we can sort it all out...

TEA, THE DRINK, AND QUEEN CATHERINE

In 1660 the English Civil War ended, and the monarchy was restored. Charles II took the throne and, two years later, he took a bride. Catherine de Braganza, daughter of the King of Portugal came to take up residence with her new husband and king. When her ship landed at the British port her Royal Highness sorely needed some refreshment and asked for a cup of tea.

To her shock, no one was able to locate even a single tea leaf to brew her a cuppa. Instead, they offered her an ale. Being a gracious Royal, she thanked them and drank it down, all the while wondering what barbaric country she had landed in.

She pondered this on the carriage ride to the castle which would be her new home. In her room, she nervously paced the floor while her maids unpacked the possessions she had brought with her. She breathed a sigh of relief when she spotted what she was looking for. In among her silk gowns and jewels, she had tucked a tin of tea leaves and some porcelain cups. She immediately sent a maid to the kitchen to brew her a cup of tea. How could she handle this new life without her tea?

Catherine was used to her daily cuppa because Portugal had a trade agreement with China which allowed them to import tea and porcelain. But, as she soon found out, England didn't have any such agreement, and tea was prohibitively expensive and rarely drunk.

The small tin of tea Catherine had brought got her through the wedding. After the ceremony, a messenger was to be sent back to the King of Portugal. He would then dispatch several ships loaded with luxurious and expensive gifts as the new Queen's dowry. But before the messenger went off, Catherine slipped him a note for her father: "Be sure to send lots of tea." Fortunately, her father obliged, and several trunks of tea leaves soon arrived for Catherine.

With her tea supply secured, Catherine was confident she could handle anything her new life might throw her way. The new Queen was considered exotic, and everyone wanted to emulate her dress, hairstyle, and even her tea habit. It became a custom among the rich ladies of the court to have a cup of tea with the Queen. A few years later, England began importing tea and the tea-drinking custom took hold among the upper classes.

AFTERNOON TEA AND THE DUCHESS OF BEDFORD

By the mid 1800s, tea was an affordable drink that could be enjoyed by all, but the word "tea" soon took on a second meaning.

In 1831 Anna Maria Russell, Duchess of Bedford, became Queen Victoria's Lady of the Bedchamber. She ate her meals at the appointed time of the court like everyone else. They ate a light lunch at midday and then dinner was served around 8 pm. That left a long gap between meals, and the Duchess often found herself feeling a bit peckish around 4:00 in the afternoon. So, to calm her grumbling tummy, she would have a tray of tea, bread and butter, sandwiches, and cake brought to her room.

This became her habit, and she enjoyed it so much, she began inviting friends around to join her for her "afternoon tea." When the Queen joined the gathering, everybody wanted in on it. The light meal became known as afternoon tea and was soon copied by other socialites. It became a ritual for the upper class and turned into a formal occasion. Ladies would change into their best gowns, gloves, and hats for afternoon tea.

The tradition of having an afternoon tea has stood the test of time. Today many people partake of it in various forms. It can be as simple as a cup of tea and a biscuit at home, or you can go out to a restaurant for a much fancier version.

Many hotels and restaurants serve quite substantial afternoon teas. They usually consist of a tiered tray of finger sandwiches, scones with clotted cream and jam, various little cakes. And, of course, tea. Champagne is often an option and going out for afternoon tea is a special treat.

PINKIES DOWN

When you go out for that special afternoon tea, you want to sip your tea properly. And that means pinkies down. Some people might think it's a sign of refinement to point their pinky finger into the air when holding a teacup, but, actually, it's not. Extended pinkies look a bit pretentious, but there's a more disturbing story behind the gesture.

It's said that the custom began during the 17th century in the French court of Louis XIV. The courtiers were pretty promiscuous, and syphilis ran rampant among them. One of the effects of this disease is the stiffening of finger joints, and after a while, the pinky will no longer bend. So when the syphilitic courtiers lifted a cup to their lips, their permanently pointing pinky stuck up in the air. Since they were the trendsetters of the day, everyone imitated them and began pointing their pinky. Since I can only assume you don't want to look pretentious or syphilitic, keep those pinkies down.

HIGH TEA AND THE WORKING CLASS

Now that we know how to hold our cups, let's move on to another tea called high tea. Traditionally high tea was a working-class dinner. While the upper crust had time to sip tea and eat dainty sandwiches in the afternoon, those working for their living didn't have that luxury.

The common folk had their tea later in the day, after they had finished work around 6:00 or so. It was also their dinner and usually consisted of bread, vegetables, cheese, and meat, all washed down with a cup of tea. In some parts of the UK, dinner is still called tea.

One theory about the names of these repasts comes from the height of the tables around which they were enjoyed. High tea was eaten by the working classes at their dinner table, and low tea (or afternoon tea) was often served on lower coffee tables in luxurious salons.

NOT TO CONFUSE THE MATTER BUT...

Some countries, including the United States, refer to afternoon tea as high tea—possibly because afternoon tea seems high class. Whatever the reason, a few hotels, mainly in London, might list their afternoon tea as high tea to cater to their, mostly foreign, clients.

Just to be clear:

- **Tea** could be a drink, an afternoon snack, or an evening meal.
- **Afternoon tea** (also referred to simply as tea) could be a snack of tea and biscuits or a light meal with sandwiches, scones, and cake.
- **High tea** (or simply tea) could be dinner or an afternoon tea in a London hotel.

So if you are ever invited to tea in England, be prepared for anything... Not really, just note the time of day, and that should clue you in on what you'll be having.

FISH AND CHIPS

A MATCH MADE IN ENGLAND

Fish and Chips. This tasty twosome has been a British favorite since the Victorian times. However, they weren't always a duo. They came to the UK separately: One hailed from Belgium and the other from Portugal, and they weren't paired up until about 1860.

Like much of history, there are several stories relating who did what first, but below is my favorite...

CHIPS

Let's start with the history of those chunky chips. They are similar to French fries but thicker and not to be confused with American-style potato chips (which are called crisps in the UK).

The British chip can trace its history back to the 1600s in Belgium. It seems that the people living along the Meuse River used to catch small fish and fry them up as a tasty addition to their meals. But one winter when it was so cold that the river froze over, an anonymous housewife got creative. If she couldn't get any fish to fry up, she would just make her own.

She searched the kitchen for dinner ideas, but all she found was potatoes. As she glanced back and forth between the spuds and her frying pan, she had an idea. If she cut the potatoes into strips about as wide as those little fish, her husband and kids might not even notice the difference. So that's what she did and *voilà*! Chips were born. (History doesn't tell us whether or not her family noticed.)

Her new culinary creation was tasty, and she told other Belgian housewives about it. Soon, the secret was out, and chips became a popular fish substitute in many homes. When the Belgian Huguenots were fleeing persecution in the seventeenth century, many of them came to London and brought their chip-frying knowledge with them.

FISH

One hundred years before the Huguenots and their chips sought refuge in London another group of persecuted people had introduced fried fish. The recipe for battered and fried fish came to London in the sixteenth century with the Sephardic Jews who were fleeing the Inquisition in Spain and Portugal.

FISH AND CHIPS

Fried fish and fried chips were both being sold in the streets of London in 1860—just not together. The idea for pairing them up came from thirteen-year-old Joseph Malin. Joseph's family was descended from those early Sephardic Jewish immigrants. The Malins were rug weavers who also sold chips from their East London home.

Little Joseph must have been eating a piece of fried fish from a neighboring shop when he popped one of his mum's chips in his mouth. He liked the combination and thought they might sell well together. It's easy to imagine him walking the streets with a tray hung round his neck calling out in his East London cockney accent, "Fish 'n' chips! Get yer fish 'n' chips 'ere, mate!"

Once people tasted fish and chips together, it was love at first bite. Joe continued selling the delicious duo on the street from his tray, and when he was a bit older, he opened a shop on Cleveland Street.

EVERYONE LOVES IT

The new pairing was a great success. Originally fish and chips were gobbled up by the lower classes. It was a cheap and filling meal—and, as an extra bonus, it tasted good. During the Industrial Revolution, it became a favorite meal of the working class and has continued climbing its way up the social ladder. Today you can find it served in posh restaurants as well as at your local chippy.

By 1910 there were more than 25,000 chippies (fish and chip shops) around the country. In the 1920s the number peaked at around 35,000. Today fish and chips has to compete with other takeaway fast foods and the number of shops has dropped to around 10,500.

WRAP IT IN NEWSPAPER

Many people remember eating takeaway fish and chips wrapped in newspaper. However, this is no longer done. It was discontinued in the 1980s for safety reasons when it was discovered that eating food covered in newspaper ink wasn't good for us. Now the dish is usually served on a plate or in a takeaway box. This makes it easier to add the customary side of mushy peas, which are similar to mashed potatoes—except they are mashed peas. The Brits often top it all off with good doses of salt and vinegar.

So, our story, which started with persecution and displacement, has a fairy-tale ending. The unlikely couple—Belgian chips and Portuguese fish—lived a long and happy life together in the UK.

BRITISH CUISINE

AMERICANS, BRITS, AND FOOD

*a*s an American, I was confused by the names of some British foods. Sometimes I would think I knew what I was getting but it would turn out to be something entirely different. This is because Brits and Americans often use the same word to mean different things. At other times, the weird and wonderful names given to British dishes conjure up images that don't necessarily make your mouth water (*toad in the hole* and *spotted dick* for example).

Since dessert is my favorite part of any meal, it's as good a place to start as any. I'm a rather picky eater, but I rarely meet a dessert that I don't like. In Britain, dessert might be called **afters**, **pudding** (or **pud** for short), or **sweet**. ("Sweets" in the plural are candies.)

American Pudding = British Custard
British Pudding = American Dessert

Our first year in England, as Christmas was approaching, I kept hearing people talk about **Christmas pudding**. They made sounds and gestures that made it seem delicious. I didn't know what it was, but I imagined it was some sort of custard—like what we call pudding in America. I couldn't wait to try this very special dessert.

When I finally saw Christmas pudding on a restaurant menu, I was thrilled and ordered it. The waiter sat it in front of me and I eyed it suspiciously. I said, "No, I ordered Christmas pudding." He assured me that it was indeed Christmas pudding, and I said, "But this isn't pudding at all —it's fruitcake." That was when I learned that pudding was a general term used for any kind of dessert. I have to admit that I was a bit disappointed in my Christmas "pudding."

Here are some other British foods with confusing and sometimes amusing names:

Chips – British **fries** are called **chips** and are usually larger, more like potato wedges. And American potato **chips** are called **crisps**.

Toad in the hole – If you're expecting a frog, you'll be disappointed. It's simply a **banger** (big sausage) with batter around it, but the name conjures up an interesting image.

Bubble and squeak – This is one of my favorite food names because it's so descriptive. It's made by frying up leftovers and is usually eaten for breakfast. Traditionally it has a base of cabbage or potatoes but any leftover veggies can be added. You can also add a bit of meat if desired. While cooking, the mixture bubbles and squeaks, just like the name implies.

Cornish Pasty – Pasty rhymes with nasty, but it tastes pretty nice if you get a good one. It's a circle of pastry, folded in half and filled with various fillings, mostly meat and potatoes. The best ones are found in Cornwall where they originated.

Curry – Britain is chock-a-block with Indian restaurants and the Indian curry has become a staple for many Brits. A curry is a dish with curry sauce and there are all types from very mild to mouth burners.

Fairy Cake – This is a wonderful name for **cupcake**. Can't you just imagine those little winged fairies eating them?

Gateau – This is the French word for cake, still used in England.

Jelly – In Britain, **jelly** can be what Americans call **jello**. No wonder the Brits aren't keen to try a peanut butter and jelly sandwich. Can you imagine peanut butter wobbling around on jello? But there's also another product called jelly in the UK which is the same as American jelly: It's jam with the pieces of fruit strained out.

Lemonade – If you order lemonade in Britain, you will be served a Sprite, 7-Up, or something similar.

Marmite – They say you either love it or hate it. I am in the latter category. It is a yeast paste with a strong salty taste, and it's usually spread on toast.

Mushy Peas – These are just what they sound like: Mashed peas with butter. They're normally served with fish and chips.

Spotted dick – This one is not at all what it sounds like: It's a suet cake containing raisins or currants, which represent the "spotted" part of the name. No one knows exactly why it is called "dick."

Yorkshire Pudding – This is not a dessert even though it's called pudding. It's more of a pastry or bread that's usually served with a roast.

Who would have thought that food could be so confusing and amusing?

III

MYSTERIES AND
CURIOSITIES

PUZZLING PERPLEXITIES

Fairies
Green People
Stone Circles
and Crop Circles

LOOKING FOR FAIRIES
AMONG THE BLUEBELLS

WATCH OUT FOR THOSE MISCHIEVOUS
LITTLE PIXIES

*E*ngland is full of fairy folk, and many of them live in ancient woodlands among the bluebells—at least that's what I had been told. And the first time I saw a bluebell wood in full bloom, I couldn't help but believe it.

My husband and I were driving along in a rural area in early spring, when I spotted a small patch of blue on the roadside. My heart skipped a beat. I began slapping my husband's arm and saying, "Pull over, pull over." He didn't know what was going on, but as soon as the car came to a stop, I jumped out and ran back to investigate. Sure enough, it was a little clump of dainty blue bell-shaped flowers. It was bluebell season!

I had seen photos of great swaths of bluebells covering a woodland floor, and I knew I had to find one. I longed to experience the magical sight that I had, up until then, only seen in photos. So I looked up the Woodland Trust website to find a bluebell wood nearby. As it turned out, we weren't far from one.

The UK has many ancient woods—a wood known to have been in existence at least since 1600. Many of them are also bluebell woods, and in the spring, when the blue flowers bloom, they take on an otherworldly feel and fragrance. This transformation has led to much folklore about fairies living among bluebells. So, while I wanted to see the masses of blue flowers, I also hoped to catch a glimpse of a fairy.

BLUEBELLS AND FAIRIES

The magical sight of a woodland carpeted with bluebells could convince anyone that it's inhabited by fairies. Nowadays, we tend to think of fairies as nice little Tinker Bell type creatures, but they haven't always enjoyed such a good reputation. In days gone by, they were considered mischievous and sometimes downright evil.

This is why you should proceed into a bluebell wood with caution. It's said that the sight and smell of these flowers are so overwhelming that they can cause an adult to be "pixie-led." That's when you go into a trance and the fairies lead you around... and around... and around... in circles until someone finds and rescues you. The fate of children is worse though: They could be abducted by fairies and never seen again. (Yikes!)

DON'T TREAD ON THE BLUEBELLS

If you do decide to venture into a bluebell wood—and you definitely should—never pick, or step on, a bluebell. This is because the fairies hang their spells on the flowers and if you break their spells, the little spirits get very upset.

The bell-shaped flowers have another use too: They ring to call the mischievous pixies to their balls and important gatherings. These bells are normally only heard by fairy ears, but if a human should ever hear them, something bad will happen to him.

So gather up your courage and visit a bluebell wood. Just remember to stay on the path and don't pick any flowers. Another reason to avoid picking them, besides not wishing to annoy the fairies, is that bluebells are poisonous. This fact might account for the many old stories warning people away from them. These days, there's an additional deterrent: Bluebells are a protected species and picking them is against the law.

BLUEBELL LORE

Even though most of the folklore about bluebells warns us to leave them alone, in one instance we are advised to pick one —and only one—then say, "Bluebell, bluebell, bring me some luck before tomorrow night." Then put the flower in your shoe and you'll have good luck—or at least a sweet-smelling foot.

In other lore, if you wear a garland of bluebells around your neck, you cannot tell a lie. And if you can manage to turn a bluebell inside out without tearing it, you'll find your true love. Bluebells planted by your front door are supposed to be good luck because if someone unwanted comes, they'll ring to warn you.

Now you might be wondering if I happened upon any fairies on my foray into the bluebells.

Sadly, no. I didn't see a single little pixie. I was just so overcome by the beauty and the sweet fragrance that time seemed to stand still. I wandered around... and around... and around... in circles until my husband came to rescue me.

- If you want to find a bluebell wood near you in April or May (depending on the weather), have a look at the Woodland Trust website: woodlandtrust. org.uk.

THE GREEN CHILDREN OF WOOLPIT
ALIENS, FOLKLORE, OR FLEMISH?

One English mystery that has yet to be solved comes from the little East Anglian town of Woolpit. As the story goes, in the twelfth century, two very odd visitors arrived. It was harvest time and the reapers were out in the fields with their scythes cutting the barley. They were surprised when they looked up and saw two children emerge from one of the ancient cavities, called wolf pits. There was a girl, maybe around ten years old, and a slightly younger boy.

The children seemed dazed and disoriented as they came stumbling through the field. One of the workers put down his scythe and went to see if they were okay. But he gasped and stepped back when he got a good look at them. From a distance they had the appearance of normal children but up close, he could see that their skin was light green. Their clothes were also strange and made of a fabric that no one had ever seen before. And they spoke a peculiar language that no one understood.

The farmers all gathered around gawking at the children. They didn't know what to make of the pair and decided to take them to the local squire. Sir Richard was a well-traveled man, and he would know where they had come from and what to do with them. Everyone was bewildered and a bit afraid of these green children, and the feeling was mutual. The youngsters were frightened by the white-skinned people babbling away at them in meaningless sounds. They began to cry. Sir Richard decided they must be hungry and offered them food, but they refused everything.

They were taken outside to Sir Richard's garden while the adults discussed what to do. When the children caught sight of some bean plants, they went wild with delight. They grabbed the stalks and tore them open, but on finding no beans, they began to cry. Someone opened a pod and showed them the beans which they immediately gobbled up. For months, they would eat only beans.

The children stayed on with Sir Richard, but the boy was sickly, and soon died. The girl flourished, however. She learned to eat normal British food and lost her green color.

THEIR STORY

Little by little the girl learned to speak English, and everyone was eager to hear her story. Where had she come from and how did she end up in East Anglia? She told them she and her brother had come from a land called St. Martin. There, everyone had green-tinged skin. It was a land with no sun, but they had a light similar to the twilight in England. From its shores they could see a land with light, but they were separated from it by a wide river.

One day, when she and her brother were out tending their flock of sheep, they saw a cave. When they peeked inside, they heard bells tinkling. Of course, they wanted to see where the sound was coming from, so they ventured inside. As they followed the sound of the bells, they went deeper and deeper into the cave. Finally, they saw light and stepped out the other end of the cave into the blinding sunlight. They couldn't see anything and fell into one of the old wolf pits. They slept there until they were awakened by the noise of the harvesters in the field.

They climbed out of the pit to look for the cave, but they couldn't find it. And that's when the harvesters found them and took them to Sir Richard.

As the girl grew up, she was no longer green and looked like the other local lasses. She worked for Sir Richard and was said to be "rather loose and wanton in her conduct." She eventually married, but we don't know whether she had any green children of her own.

Could this be a true story? Well, there does seem to be some basis of truth to it. This story was related by two medieval writers: William of Newburgh wrote about it in the 12th century and cited "trustworthy" sources. Then Ralph of Coggeshall wrote about the matter and listed Sir Richard de Cain (the squire with whom the children lived) as a source.

ALIEN, FOLKLORE, OR FLEMISH?

There are several theories about where these green children might have come from: Some claim that the story is just a bit of folklore and the green children were no more real than

Little Red Riding Hood or Hansel and Gretel. Others see them as alien visitors from another planet.

However, there's another theory: Maybe they were Flemish. In the town of Fornham St. Martin (also in East Anglia) there was a large settlement of Flemish weavers. In 1173 the area around this town was the site of a major battle and many of the Flemish immigrants were killed. Perhaps the children's parents died at that time and they fled and got lost in the woods. After wandering for days, they ended up in Woolpit. Their color could be explained by a dietary deficiency disease called chlorosis, also known as green sickness. And if their parents were weavers it could account for their strange clothes.

The story of the green children of Woolpit has been told and retold for centuries, and we'll probably never solve the mystery of who they were or where they came from, but the Flemish theory sounds quite plausible.

- Woolpit is a village in the county of Suffolk in the East of England. It's about two hours northeast of London or about one hour east of Cambridge.

A STONEHENGE STORY

HOW TO MOVE A MONUMENT

*S*tonehenge presents us with another unsolved mystery. It's an impressive sight, and as you gaze upon it, you can't help but wonder how ancient people built this incredible monument. How did they manage to put those gigantic stones on top of one another?

People in the Middle Ages were wondering the same thing. And just like today, they came up with their own theory. As far as we know, Geoffrey of Monmouth was the first person to write a story explaining the origin of Stonehenge, and according to him, the credit goes to Merlin, the wizard from the tales of King Arthur.

BRITAIN NEEDS A MONUMENT

The story goes something like this… It was a terrible time in Britain. The Saxons had ravaged the land and killed 3,000 nobles. The new King Aurelius, who was the future King Arthur's uncle, was distressed. He wanted to build a monument on Salisbury Plain which was the burial site of those who had been slain. He brought together the royal architects, but they couldn't come up with any suitable ideas.

Then someone suggested to the King that he consult Merlin, who was known throughout the land for his wisdom and his knowledge of the mechanical arts. So the king sent for him and explained what he wanted.

MERLIN HAS AN IDEA

Merlin scratched his head and had a think. Then he said, "Yes, I know just the thing. In Ireland, on top of Mount Killaraus, there's a monument that would be perfect. It's called Giant's Dance, and it's a circle formed of huge stones built by a giant who lived there long ago. He came from Africa and brought the boulders with him."

"Hang on a minute," said the King laughing. "Why would we go all the way to Ireland for stones? Don't we have plenty of them here in Britain? They're lying all around us."

"These are special stones," Merlin continued. "They have healing powers. The priests in Ireland wash these stones and collect the water as it runs off. The water takes on the healing virtue of the stones, and they pour it into tubs. Anyone with any kind of ailment who bathes in that water will be healed. The stones also possess a kind of magic that will preserve the memory of our dead. And if this monument is set up here in Britain, it will last forever."

The king agreed that it did indeed sound like a fitting monument. Merlin warned him that the stones were pretty big so he would need some strong men. The King sent an army of 15,000 men with Merlin and Uther Pendragon (the future King Arthur's father) to Ireland to collect the stones. After a little run-in with the local king, who didn't want a British army on his soil or taking his stones, the Brits arrived at the monument they had come for.

HOW TO MOVE A MONUMENT

The stones were much larger than the soldiers had been expecting, and they stood gaping at them in awe. But they were all strong young men, so if anyone could move those stones, they could. Merlin smiled at them, then told them to go ahead and move the stones by whatever means they could. The men used ropes, levers, pulleys, and lots of brute strength, but not one stone budged.

When they were all exhausted and out of ideas, they just gave up and sat down on the ground. Merlin walked into the center of the stone circle and paced around muttering to himself. Then he rearranged all the ropes, pulleys, and levers and told the men to try again. To their amazement, this time they easily dislodged the stones and moved them to the ship.

When they reached Britain, they used Merlin's same techniques to transport the stones to the Salisbury plain. They arranged them there just like they had been in Ireland.

Stonehenge was the result. It was a fitting memorial to the dead and a reminder that while you can do a lot with brute strength, it takes brains to move a monument.

TODAY'S THEORY

While today's researchers reject the Merlin theory, they still can't be sure how these massive stones were moved. The large ones, which average 25 tons each, were brought from about 20 miles away. The smaller ones, weighing between two and five tons each, came from the mountains of Southwest Wales more than 150 miles away.

The modern theory is that the boulders were transported by water and then by land. And to move one stone, it probably took more than 100 people and a system of sledges or wooden rollers.

It sounds to me like they needed Merlin!

- Stonehenge is near Amesbury, Wiltshire, SP4 7DE. It's about two hours west of London or one hour south east of Bath.
- Avebury - About 25 miles north of Stonehenge is another henge made of stone. There was a stone circle at Avebury which was larger than Stonehenge. Unfortunately, many of the stones were broken up and reused. However, it's still quite impressive and, unlike Stonehenge, you can get as close as you want and touch the ancient stones.

BRITISH CROP CIRCLES

THEIR MYSTERY AND THEIR HISTORY

*C*rop circles are both a curiosity and a mystery. While some are definitely human-made, others are of questionable origin. These intricate designs appear sporadically worldwide, but southwest England seems to be the epicenter of crop circle activity. Those curious formations began to make headlines in the 1970s. That's when quite a few of them started springing up overnight in the fields of Wiltshire in southwest England.

This is the land of Stonehenge and other mysterious ancient formations. And it's also a place where many claim to have seen UFOs or strange balls of light in the sky. So, right away, there was speculation about aliens or mystical forces.

At first the formations were just circles made from plants which were bent flat to the ground with all the stalks pointing in the same direction. They looked very much like the landing place of a flying saucer. As time went on, the patterns became more and more intricate, and people surmised that the "others" were sending us coded messages.

Crop circles were mysterious and no one knew where they came from or what they meant.

SCIENTISTS VS BELIEVERS

As each new crop circle was reported, people flocked to the Wiltshire countryside to see them. Scientists tried to find the cause of the strange formations. They had their theories: The circles could be formed by small whirlwinds, or possibly by some magnetic field running under the earth's surface.

Meanwhile others, whom we'll call "believers," were certain they were supernatural. They came to try and understand their meaning and to feel the power said to be within them. The believers had their theories as well: The simple circles could be where a UFO had landed. The more complicated designs could be messages from a higher intelligence— possibly aliens, or other spiritual beings.

HOAXERS

The mystery seemed to be solved in 1991, when two men came forward to claim responsibility. It was all a hoax. Doug Bower and Dave Chorley said they had been fooling the public with their designs since 1978. They met with reporters, told their story, explained how they made the circles, and even gave a demonstration.

Doug and Dave were friends who often met for a pint and a chat. One evening Dave recalled a story he had heard when he was in Australia: In the 1960s a flattened circle had been discovered in a reed bed, and the locals were sure it had been made by a flying saucer. It made the news and stirred up a lot of controversy.

As the two men gazed out the pub window over a wheat field, they had an idea. If they were to make a circle like that in England, would people attribute it to a UFO as well? They thought it would be a good laugh, so they started making a plan. They set a date, and in the middle of the night, they met in a local field for their trial run. They took a long metal pole and knocked down the stalks into a nice neat circle. But to their dismay, no one noticed. So they made a few more, but still, their circles got no attention. They continued trying off and on for two years.

Finally, Doug and Dave decided their circles weren't visible enough. So they made an eighty-foot-wide circle that could be seen from a hilltop that was popular with tourists. The next day, their circle was national news. The press showed up to take photos and conduct interviews, scientists came to investigate, and the believers came to marvel at the mystery.

The two men got a kick out of all the attention, especially when they read that the crop circle might have been made by a "higher intelligence." This fueled their desire to make more circles and fool more people. And just to be sure they weren't wasting their time, they introduced themselves to some of the investigators. They said they were nature enthusiasts who knew the area well, and they volunteered to notify them if they spotted any new formations.

In 1991 Doug and Dave called it quits and decided to hang up their circle-making hats. They came clean and told their story to the papers. They demonstrated how they had made the crop circles by using a simple board with a rope tied to each end to walk out the designs. As further proof, they revealed drawings of all their designs. They claimed to have made all the circles in the area between 1978 and 1987. After that it seems they had competition from imitators. But they still claimed more than 200 during their years of activity from 1978 to 1991.

The confession seemed to settle the crop circle conundrum. It had all been a big hoax. The designs had simply been made by pranksters going out into the fields under the cover of darkness and flattening crops...

Or had it?

EARLIER CROP CIRCLES

As soon as the story appeared in the newspapers, local people began to write in. Many said they had seen circles in the crops long before 1978 when the two men had begun their little joke. People even remembered their parents and grandparents talking about them. The older generation usually explained the circles as being the result of small whirlwinds.

But these earlier crop circles didn't attract any media attention. To the local farmers, they were just a part of farming. So, while many crop circles were definitely made by humans and had been explained by the pranksters, it seemed that there were other ones, even older, which were still a mystery.

DID THE DEVIL DO IT?

The earliest published record of what might be considered a crop circle is a seventeenth-century pamphlet squarely placing the blame on the Devil. It tells of a farmer who had a field of oats ready for cutting. He was bargaining with a poor mower, but when the mower asked too much money for the job, the farmer declared, "I'd rather have the Devil mow it than you."

That night the field began to glow and looked like it was on fire. Many of the locals saw the blazes from afar. The farmer had also seen the flames, so the next morning, when he went to look at his field, he expected his crop to be burned to cinders. But instead, his oats were all neatly mown and every stalk was facing the same direction. The townsfolk decided that no human could have done it: It must have been the Devil.

The account says the oats weren't cut in the usual way, the Devil had *"cut them in round circles, and plac't every straw with that exactness that it would have taken up above an age for any man to perform what he did that one night."* It was so mysterious that the farmer was afraid to move them...

Could this seventeenth-century tale be describing a crop circle?

FARMERS

While scientists and believers love crop circles and can't wait to see the next one, some farmers are getting downright angry. As the designs get larger and larger, more of their crops are being destroyed: first within the design of the crop circles, then by those who tramp through the fields to see them.

Certain landowners are demanding that crop circle makers and tourists stop trespassing on their land and destroying their property. But other farmers have decided to go with the flow and cash in on the crop circle craze: They've begun to charge an entrance fee to see the designs which appear on their property.

So, whether you are a scientist, a believer, or just curious, if you go to the countryside this summer in search of crop circles, please be respectful of the farmers who are trying to make a living with these crops.

––––––––––––

- You can visit the Crop Circle Exhibition & Information Centre at Honeystreet Mill Cafe, Honeystreet, Pewsey, Wiltshire, SN9 5PS. They should have details about which farmers have given permission for access and sometimes you can make a donation at the Centre to the ones you visit.

IV

REMNANTS OF RELIGION

TEMPLES, CHURCHES, AND MIRACLES

Ancient Curses
Medieval Church Carvings
and Legends

CURSES IN THE TEMPLE
BATHING AND CURSING LIKE A
ROMAN IN BATH

The city of Bath in southwest England is named after the Roman bath that was built there in the first century AD. However, when the Romans arrived, there was already a temple on the site of the bubbling hot spring. The locals had long considered it a sacred place and had dedicated it to their mother goddess, Sulis.

Of course, the mighty Romans wanted to build something bigger and better. They constructed a new temple and, since Sulis was similar to their goddess, Minerva, they decided they were one and the same. They dedicated their new temple to Sulis Minerva. Then they built an elaborate bathhouse complex containing multiple rooms: changing room, hot pool, cold plunge pool, warm soaking pool, and a sauna. The Romans loved to luxuriate in their baths and could spend most of the day there. It was a long, luxurious experience, and at the end of it, they should have been as mellow as a meditating monk.

But every now and then...

A smiling Roman comes out of the spa all relaxed and feeling great—then he goes into the changing room to get dressed. He looks in the corner where he left his toga and his smile fades. It's not there. He was a little short on cash this week, so he didn't hire anyone to guard it. His blood pressure starts to rise as he searches the room. It's gone. Now he's furious and his blood pressure is through the roof. All the benefits of his relaxing bath are down the drain.

But he knows just what to do. He'll curse the person who took his toga. But first he has to send someone out to the forum to buy him some new threads. Then, grumbling to himself, he heads to the temple of the goddess Sulis Minerva which is attached to the baths. He goes straight to the basket of curse tablets which is filled with small, thin squares of soft lead. He buys one and furiously begins to scratch words into it:

To the powerful and righteous Sulis Minerva,
I dedicate my best toga to you, and I ask you to punish the person who stole it from me today. Make him unable to sleep or eat until he returns it. Make his hair and teeth fall out. Give him a nasty, itchy rash. And anything else you deem appropriate. I think it might have been: Domitius, Cassius, Vitus, or Octavius. They are all jealous of me, so you should look at them first. If it's not one of them, then punish whoever stole it. Show no mercy until my toga is returned.
All my best,
Your loyal follower,
Antonius

Then he folds the soft lead tablet and throws it into the sacred spring located inside the temple. That should do it.

But now he has to go home and explain to his wife why he's wearing a new outfit. And all he wanted was a relaxing day at the baths to forget his troubles...

THE REAL CURSES

During an excavation under the Roman baths in 1979, archaeologists found 130 curse tablets dating from the 2nd to the 4th century AD. They were mostly written to curse people who had stolen something. The Romans could curse anyone for anything, but the curse tablets at Bath are mostly for stolen items.

Some of the curses found in Bath:

- This curse is for the person who stole *vilbia* (it's unclear who or what *vilbia* is). Then the writer gives a list of 10 possible suspects.
- Curse for the person who stole a cloak and bathing tunic.
- A list of names—possible thieves for the goddess to investigate.
- Solinus to the goddess Sulis Minerva: "I give to your divinity and majesty my bathing tunic and cloak. Do not allow sleep or health to him ...who has done me wrong, whether man or woman, whether slave or free, unless he reveals himself and brings those goods to your temple."

CURSE WRITING FOR DUMMIES

The curses seem to follow a formula, so maybe there was a helpful curse-writing handbook near the pool:

Step one: Give the stolen item to the goddess Sulis Minerva.

Step two: Ask her to punish the person who stole the item from you (and now her). List various terrible things you want her to do to them.

Step three: Give the goddess the name of the thief or a list of possible suspects so she'll have something to go on. If you don't have any idea who stole your stuff, you make sure no one escapes the goddess's investigation by adding "whether man or woman, boy or girl, slave or free…"

Step four: Fold or roll up the curse and throw it into the sacred spring.

*To make the magic even stronger you could write backwards or add magic words or symbols.

Wow! I'm glad there's now a modern spa in Bath. It has everything the Romans had with the addition of nice secure lockers. We can have the Roman bath experience and be pretty sure our clothes will be waiting for us, right where we left them.

- In 2014 the Bath curse tablets were inscribed on the UNESCO Memory of the World UK register.
- The Roman Baths are located in the old town center next to Bath Abbey: Abbey Church Yard, Bath BA1 1LZ.
- Today you can even drink the Bath water. In the Pump Room restaurant next to the baths you can sample the mineral water that comes directly from the spring—and it's guaranteed to be curse-free.

THE MYSTERIOUS GREEN MEN IN MEDIEVAL CHURCHES
WHO ARE THEY AND WHAT DO THEY MEAN?

*I*f you enter one of the magnificent British churches or cathedrals built during the Middle Ages and feel like you're being watched—you probably are. And not just by the gargoyles, grotesques, and other obvious carvings. Look up toward the ceiling and you might see a man's face peeking out from an entanglement of leaves—as if he is hiding and wants to observe you undetected.

WHO ARE THOSE GREEN MEN?

These curious characters that inhabit our sacred spaces are called Green Men and they come in all shapes and sizes. Sometimes they just stare stoically at us, but often they taunt us by making faces or sticking out their tongues. At other times they're busy spewing foliage out of their mouths, ears, and even their eyes. What these strange faces might have meant to our medieval ancestors remains unknown.

They're called "Green Men" with the "green" part of their name referring to the vegetation surrounding (and sometimes sprouting from) their heads. Very rarely, you might find a green woman or a green animal, but for the most part, they are masks of men who have beards and hair made of leaves. They might be carved of stone or wood and they usually gaze down from church ceilings or pose at the top of columns.

The Green Man's history is long and obscure. Examples of foliage-covered faces were found in ancient Roman times, and they began to crop up in European churches in the first few centuries AD. But they reached their zenith during the Middle Ages, when there was a surge in church and cathedral building.

WHAT DO THEY MEAN?

Unfortunately, medieval architects left no record of who these Green Men were or what they might represent. Nor do we find any clues in church archives. With no firm trail of evidence to tell us who or what they are, people have attached their own ideas to them.

Pagan God

To some people, the Green Man appears to be a Pagan symbol. Perhaps he had links to the Greek god, Dionysus (also called Bacchus by the Romans) who was god of wine, fertility, and religious ecstasy. Bacchus was often represented wearing a wreath of vines and leaves.

Tree Worship

Another hypothesis is that the Green Man was an integration of tree worship into the church. We know that some Pagans worshipped trees and that in the early days of Christianity, Pagans were brought into the fold by incorporating some of their familiar customs and symbols. Could the Green Man be a tree or vegetation deity?

Personification of Nature

Others think that the Green Man might just be a personification of nature. Some Green Men are surrounded by spring leaves and others by autumn foliage. So maybe he's simply the face of nature and the changing seasons which represent birth, death, and rebirth.

Whatever these Green Men represented, they didn't cause a fuss with medieval churchgoers. No one ever bothered to explain them, and it seems that no one objected to them either. They were simply part of church decoration.

LADY RAGLAN NAMES THE GREEN MAN

In the late nineteenth and early twentieth century, an interest in folklore and ancient customs took root. People wanted to preserve the old ideas and stories before they were lost to the modern world. And along came Lady Raglan...

Julia Raglan considered herself an amateur folklorist. She was the wife of Lord Raglan who also dabbled in anthropology and archaeology.

One day Lady Raglan was visiting a church in Wales and the minister, who also fancied himself a student of folklore, pointed out a carving in the church. It was a man's face with oak leaves growing out of the mouth and ears. The minister suggested that it might represent the spirit of inspiration.

But Lady Raglan had other ideas. She began to think of pagan religions and other folkloric characters that she had been reading about. She concluded that the church carvings, along with several mythic characters such as Robin Hood, Jack in the Green, and the May King, must all be representations of the same early pagan deity—which she dubbed the Green Man.

She published her article, *The Green Man in Church Architecture*, in *Folklore Magazine* in 1939. This article popularized the term "Green Man" for the church carvings that had previously been known as "foliate heads."

In later years, when the study of folklore and architecture was taken up by more serious scholars, Lady Raglan's theories were questioned. It seems there was no real evidence to connect Robin Hood and the other characters to the Green Men found in churches. Neither was there any proof that they had Pagan origins. But it was a good theory and there are still those who believe it today.

SECULAR ARCHITECTURE AND PUBS

During the nineteenth-century Gothic Revival, the Green Man leapt from churches over into secular architecture. Then later, when the Arts and Crafts movement came along, his leaves and nature theme meant that he fit right in with that design style too.

"Green Man" is a popular name for pubs and has been since the fifteenth century. They originally took the name from a brewing company called Green Man and Still. Their signs usually depicted a woodsman or a wild man with a club who wore green clothes or was decked in green leaves. But after the foliate heads had taken on the same name and gained popularity, many of the Green Man pubs changed their signs to a face surrounded by foliage.

Today, the Green Man is more popular than ever. To modern folk who are concerned about the environment, he's the spirit of nature and embodies the idea that man and the natural world are intertwined. He's an ancient symbol that's still relevant today, whatever you choose to believe about him.

* Green men can be found in many medieval churches throughout England. Sometimes they are difficult to spot, so you might need to ask someone to point them out. Winchester Cathedral claims to have 60 Green Men.

BUNNY WITH A BAG

DID HE INSPIRE THE ALICE IN
WONDERLAND RABBIT?

*M*edieval churches are bursting at the seams with decorative images. You'll find Green Men, gargoyles, grotesques, and it's not uncommon to see representations of animals as well. Most of them are shown doing normal animal things. However, there's an unusual carved rabbit on the wall of St. Mary's church in Beverley, England.

This rabbit is unusual because he's not running or hopping like most rabbits: He's walking upright and carrying a bag. He bears a striking resemblance to the White Rabbit in *Alice in Wonderland*, but this bunny has a story all of his own.

St. Mary's church in Beverley was founded in 1120 and this rabbit carving dates from around 1330. He's sometimes referred to as the "pilgrim" rabbit or the "messenger" rabbit because of his bag. And some say he was the inspiration for the White Rabbit in *Alice in Wonderland* and the Messenger Rabbit in *Through the Looking Glass*.

Lewis Carroll, the author of these two books, had connections to the area, as his grandparents lived close to Beverley. So, it's possible that he visited this church and the image of this "bunny with a bag" sparked his imagination.

THE WHITE RABBIT

In *Alice in Wonderland*, the White Rabbit is the first character Alice meets. He walks upright, wears a waistcoat, and carries a pocket watch. As he hurries along, he mutters, "Oh dear! Oh dear! I shall be too late!" But most of us remember the Disney rhyming version, "I'm late, I'm late, for a very important date." Alice is intrigued by the bizarre bunny and follows him down the rabbit hole where her adventures begin.

The White Rabbit's human stance is very similar to the rabbit sculpture in Beverley, but his tardiness was apparently inspired by Alice Liddell's (the real-life Alice's) father who never managed to arrive anywhere on time.

THE MESSENGER RABBIT

The rabbit in *Through the Looking Glass* is a messenger to the king. This rabbit is called Haigha, which he claims rhymes with "mayor." He dresses in medieval fashion and carries a bag—just like the Beverley bunny does.

When Alice sees Haigha coming down the road, she remarks that he has a "very curious attitude"—because he keeps "skipping up and down, and wriggling like an eel… with his great hands spread out like fans on each side."

But the King explains that "he's an Anglo-Saxon Messenger —and those are Anglo-Saxon attitudes." Later, when the King is hungry, the rabbit opens his bag and pulls out a sandwich and some hay for his Lordship's lunch.

THE PILGRIM BAG

And what about that bag slung over the Beverley Bunny's shoulder? This bag is the reason he's often identified as a pilgrim rabbit. It's called a scrip and all fashionable medieval pilgrims carried one as they traveled across the country visiting churches and praying at shrines. It held their food, money, and other essentials and was an important part of their traveling attire.

TALE OF THE BEVERLEY BUNNY

The Beverley Bunny might have inspired the rabbits in Lewis Carroll's books, but he also has a story of his own to tell. In the Middle Ages, when many people couldn't read, lessons were taught in paintings and sculptures on church walls. The priests also used fables and folk tales in their sermons to get their point across. This rabbit sculpture is a reminder of a medieval cautionary fable by Odo of Cheriton.

It's the story of the simple people of Wilby (or Wilebege). The village lay at the very limits of their lord's territory, and by the time they received their tax notice, it was late. There was no way they could get the money back to their lord on time. They were all in a tizzy. What could they do?

Then one of them came up with an idea. He said, "The rabbit is the fastest creature, so why don't we put the notice and the payment in a bag, put it on a rabbit, and send him to our lord's manor. Surely he will get there quicker than any of us could." Everyone agreed that it was quite a clever idea, so that's just what they did.

After putting the bag around the rabbit, they instructed him to run as fast as he could to their lord's manor. Then they let him go. The rabbit shot out of their hands and ran off into the forest... and neither the rabbit nor their money was ever seen again. The moral of the story: Think carefully before putting your trust and money in the hands (or paws) of a stranger.

The Beverley Bunny's story seems just about as bizarre as the stories that take place in Wonderland. So he seems a fitting model for Lewis Carroll's rabbits.

- Beverley is a town in Yorkshire in northern England. It's about an hour southeast of York.

MYTHS AND LEGENDS
OF GLASTONBURY

IS THE HOLY GRAIL HIDDEN THERE?

*G*lastonbury might just be the most mystical or spiritual place in England. It claims to be the site of the first church in the British Isles, Jesus might have visited here, it's the Isle of Avalon where King Arthur was buried, St. Patrick is buried here, the Holy Grail is buried here, there's a thorn tree that's a direct descendant of "crown of thorns" tree, and there's a hill that's a direct link to the underworld. Wow! That's almost unbelievable.

Most of these stories come down to us from the Middle Ages. And medieval storytellers were known for taking a bit of history and adding a dose of myth and a dash of legend. They mixed it all up and out came a rousing good tale. The town of Glastonbury is connected to many such tales. Let's start exploring them with the legend of Joseph of Arimathea...

JOSEPH OF ARIMATHEA AND JESUS IN ENGLAND

In the Bible, Joseph of Arimathea is mentioned as a rich man who took Jesus' body off the cross and placed it in his own tomb.

But legend fleshes out the story a bit more...

It's said that Joseph of Arimathea was Jesus' uncle. He was a businessman—a tin merchant who travelled often to Britain to visit the tin mines of Cornwall. It's even claimed that when Jesus was a young man, he might have accompanied his uncle on some of these trips and visited Glastonbury. This story is the basis for William Blake's 1808 poem *And did those feet in ancient time* which was also put to music as the anthem, *Jerusalem*.

JOSEPH AND GLASTONBURY'S OLD CHURCH

Joseph came to be associated with Glastonbury in the Middle Ages. About 50 years after the tomb of King Arthur was found at Glastonbury Abbey, the monks wrote Joseph of Arimathea into their history. Ancient legend said that their Old Church (the first church in Britain) had been founded by a disciple of Jesus. So, they thought, maybe it had been Joseph of Arimathea. Why not? It could have been him. So, they just slotted him right into their history books.

JOSEPH AND THE HOLY GRAIL

This was about the same time that the Arthurian story of Joseph of Arimathea was written. It linked together Joseph, Arthur, and the Holy Grail. The Holy Grail (or chalice) being the cup Jesus and his disciples drank from at the Last Supper.

The legend continues...

Joseph of Arimathea was a spectator at the Last Supper. He hadn't earned a seat at the table, so he had to watch from his chair off to the side. But when Jesus and his disciples got up and left the table, Joseph wandered over and picked up the cup they had drunk from and stashed it in his pocket.

Soon afterward Jesus was arrested and crucified. Joseph, who was well off and had connections, went to Pilate and asked for Jesus' body. Pilate agreed, so Joseph and his friend Nicodemus went together to take the body off the cross. While they were in the process, blood began to drip from Jesus' foot. Joseph still had the Last Supper chalice in his pocket, so he pulled it out and caught some of the blood in it.

The two men wrapped Jesus' body in sheets and laid it in the new tomb that Joseph had provided. When he got home, Joseph hid the cup under his bed. It wasn't safe to be associated with Jesus. In fact, he was arrested a few days later for taking Jesus' body—even though he had permission.

JOSEPH GOES TO JAIL

Soldiers beat him and threw him into a small building without windows. They left him there to die without food or water. But Jesus appeared to him the first night. He was holding the cup which Joseph had hidden at home—and it was glowing. Jesus left the chalice with Joseph and told him not to worry, that he would be set free when the time was right.

Every day, one wafer would appear in the cup for Joseph to eat. It wasn't much, but, miraculously, it sustained him. He stayed locked up in that building for many years, and, amazingly, when he was finally released, he was fit and healthy and hadn't aged a bit.

He took the cup and left. As soon as he got home, he began asking around for other Christians who might want to make a trip with him. They would go to Britain, a place he knew well from his days of trading in tin.

CHALICE WELL

When Joseph and his traveling party reached Britain's shores, they made their way to Glastonbury. There they established the first church in Britain. Joseph wanted to make sure the Holy Chalice was protected, so he began looking for a hiding place. He tucked it inside the mouth of a spring, and immediately the water began to run red as blood.

Today this place is called the Chalice Well or the Blood Spring. We now know that the red color comes from iron oxide in the earth, but in the Middle Ages it seemed magical. Water from the spring tastes like iron (or blood), and some say it has healing properties. Just next to the Chalice Well is the White Spring, whose calcium-rich flow leaves a white trail behind.

Back to our legend...

GLASTONBURY THORN MYTH

After Joseph and his friends safely hid away the chalice, they took a walk up a nearby small hill. When they reached the top, they were tired, and Joseph said, "Let's sit and rest, for we are weary all." He stuck his staff in the ground and they all sat down. After a chat, and maybe a little picnic, they were refreshed. They got up and walked back to the church, but Joseph was feeling so well that he forgot his walking stick.

The next day Joseph sent a young man up the hill to fetch his cane. But when he tried to pull it out of the ground, he couldn't. It had taken root. The stick had been carved from a hawthorn branch—perhaps the very tree that produced the crown of thorns. However, this new tree that sprouted from Joseph's cane wasn't a normal hawthorn. This tree bloomed twice per year: once in spring and once in winter—at Christmas time.

GLASTONBURY THORN TREE

Today, the special species of twice-blooming hawthorn can still be seen in Glastonbury. It's called the Glastonbury Thorn or the Holy Thorn. And the hill where it grew and where Joseph and his followers rested became known as Wearyall Hill—because Joseph said, "We are weary all."

The specimens of the Glastonbury Thorn growing in the town today are all claimed to be grafted from the twice-blooming original. This special tree can't be propagated by seeds or cuttings because the new plants will be normal hawthorns, blooming once per year. However, if a cutting from the Glastonbury Thorn is grafted onto regular hawthorn rootstock, it will retain its twice-blooming feature.

DESTROYED BY PURITANS

The tree on Wearyall Hill had a hard life. In the 17th century, during the English Civil War, the Puritans chopped it down and burned it. They considered it an object of superstition. It was replaced in 1951 but vandalized in 2010. Subsequent trees planted on the hill were also vandalized. Even though the original tree is long gone and there are no more trees on Wearyall Hill, descendants of the Glastonbury Thorn can still be seen around the town, including one at the abbey and one at the Church of St. John.

TALES OF THE TREE

Before being tortured and burned by the Puritans, the Holy Thorn had been able to fend for itself. One account tells of an incident when a man decided to chop it down. At the time, the tree had two trunks. The man had already cut one trunk to the ground and was about to start on the other when a branch fell and the thorns put out his eye. That would teach him. And according to the account, the part that he had already cut off continued to bloom on the ground.

It seems this Holy Thorn had a mind of its own. In September 1752, England changed from the Julian calendar to the Gregorian one. This made Christmas eleven days earlier. People wondered when the Glastonbury Thorn would bloom: Old Christmas or new Christmas? On the new Gregorian Christmas Day people gathered at the tree to see if it would bloom. It turned out that the old Thorn wasn't a fan of the new calendar. The tree simply ignored it and bloomed on the old Christmas eleven days later, January 5th.

THORN FLOWERS FOR THE QUEEN

Today, the thorn's blooming period is affected by the weather, but it does usually bloom around Christmas. Every year the students from St. John's Infants School gather around the tree and sing Christmas carols. Then the oldest child has the honor of cutting a blooming branch from the Holy Thorn tree. This branch is then sent to the Queen for her Christmas table following a tradition that began in the 1600s.

GLASTONBURY TOR

The first Holy Thorn tree grew on Wearyall Hill, but Glastonbury has a much larger hill: The Tor. Tor is a Celtic word meaning "hill," and the 500-foot tall, cone-shaped Glastonbury Tor is hard to miss. In ancient times, the plains were covered in shallow marshy water, and the tall hill was an island. This is why it's called the Isle of Avalon—or the Isle of Glass.

The Tor is crowned with the remains of a 14th-century chapel (St. Michael's tower) which was built to replace an earlier one that toppled in an earthquake in 1275. And the hill is believed to have been an ancient pagan site before that. This odd outcropping has inspired many legends. Some say the Tor is actually hollow and is a portal to the underworld and fairies. Others claim that there is some powerful magnetic force underneath it. Whatever it may be, many people enjoy the climb to see for themselves if there are any magical powers up on top of this seemingly out-of-place hill.

ST. PATRICK AT GLASTONBURY

Another thing that seems out of place in Glastonbury is St. Patrick's chapel. Everyone knows that St. Patrick was an Irish saint so why would he be here? As it turns out, Patrick was born in Britain and it's claimed that in his later years he returned—and lived in Glastonbury. He was, supposedly, buried in the Old Church in a tomb adorned with gold and silver. One source from around 1000 AD says that many Irish pilgrims came to Glastonbury to see St. Patrick's tomb. So who knows?

THE TOWN

Putting Glastonbury's ancient and mythical sites aside, it's still an interesting little town. It could be described as quirky, odd, magical, new age... The small main street is lined with shops smelling of incense and selling crystals, chimes, fairies, green men, and more. But it is probably best known for the Glastonbury Festival—a performing arts festival which takes place in the summer. Funnily enough, it isn't even in Glastonbury, it's in Pilton, another small town close by.

- Glastonbury is in the county of Somerset in southwest England. It's about three hours from London or just a bit over an hour from Bath.

V

ROYALTY

THEIR DEEDS AND MISDEEDS

*A Few Curious Kings,
Queens, and
Related Royal Things*

BLADUD: FOUNDER OF BATH
AND THE FIRST FLYING KING

*B*ladud was the legendary 9th King of the Britons. He may not be very well-known, but his feats were impressive. He's remembered for two very different reasons: First, he (and his pigs) discovered the healing powers of the warm mineral spring in Bath, England, and second, he was the first king to spread his wings and fly (as far as we know).

BLADUD IN THE BATH

The city of Bath, England is named after the Roman Baths which were built there around 60 AD. But the Romans weren't the first ones to bathe in that warm mineral spring water. According to legend, Prince Bladud had discovered that bubbling spring 900 years earlier—around 863 BC. (That's 110 years before the city of Rome was even founded.)

The first mention of King Bladud's remarkable story comes from Geoffrey of Monmouth's *History of the Kings of Britain* written in the 12th century. But there's a pretty good chance Geoffrey made up at least some of it—he was known for embellishing stories.

Over the years, the tale of Bladud, the King who founded Bath, was expanded upon and added to, and there have been many versions. Here is mine...

PRINCE BLADUD

King Ludhurdibras and his queen had a son, Prince Bladud, who was an intelligent and curious child. When he grew into a young man, his father sent him to Athens to study with the great teachers and philosophers.

Prince Bladud was enjoying his studies when he received a message that his father had died suddenly. He immediately set out for home to take up his duties as the new King of the Britons.

Unfortunately, on the ship home, he came into contact with a passenger who had an infectious skin disease. By the time Bladud reached Britain's shore, he was covered with scabs and his skin was peeling. He went to the palace walls, but dared not go inside for fear of infecting his mother. He sent a messenger with a letter for her.

His mother wept as the messenger read the note from her son. She sent a message back to him along with a gold ring and some money. "My dear son, wear this ring and I will always be able to recognize you, even if your face is disfigured."

BLADUD THE SWINEHERD

Prince Bladud kissed the ring and put it on his finger. Then he went off and bought a herd of swine. He roamed around the Avon Valley with only his pigs for company. He spent his time observing nature, contemplating the mysteries of the universe, and experimenting with plants in hope of finding a cure for his disease. But nothing worked.

One day as Bladud passed through the area now known as Bath, his pigs found acorns to eat and warm mud to wallow in. The curious prince investigated and found a hot spring bubbling up from the earth which was creating the mud. The pigs enjoyed their mud bath and came out caked in it. Overnight the mud dried, and the next morning, Bladud began to clean his pigs.

He was amazed to see that their skin was smooth. His pigs were a rowdy bunch (as most pigs are) and they were always fighting over food. All this fighting left their skin covered in cuts and scratches. But, strangely, his pigs now had smooth, healthy skin. Was he in a magical place? Could it be the mud?

If the mud had healed the pigs' skin, maybe it would heal his too. He stripped off his clothes and waded into the black goo. It was warm and squishy and made his legs tingle. So he sat down—then he lay down and rolled around making sure he was covered head to toe in the warm mud. It was so relaxing that he fell asleep and slept there all night.

When he awoke the next morning, he wiped the mud from one arm. He couldn't see any scabs. He stuck out a leg and skimmed off the muck—no scabs—no peeling skin!

He climbed out of the mire and ran to the Avon River to wash himself. As the mud slipped away, fresh, soft skin revealed itself. He laughed. He cried. He made quite a ruckus. "This is, indeed, a holy place," he shouted to his pigs. They just ignored him and continued to fight over their acorn breakfast.

Next he gave his pigs a good bath in the river, then took them to the nearest town and sold them. He got a high price because they were the finest-looking pigs anyone had ever seen. Then Prince Bladud bought the best suit of clothes in town, put them on, and headed home.

KING BLADUD

As he entered the castle and saw his mother, he held up his hand with the ring. But she didn't need the ring to recognize her son. She commanded that preparations be made to crown the new king, King Bladud, the 9th King of the Britons.

The first thing King Bladud did was to go back to the warm mud and build a temple over the hot spring. He dedicated it to the goddess Sulis, the goddess of healing and sacred waters. (And there was still a temple on that spot when the Romans arrived about 900 years later.)

King Bladud reigned for 20 years and never lost his love of learning. He summoned some of the philosophers he had studied with in Athens and they established a university north of London. He also studied magic and encouraged it throughout his kingdom.

He regularly consulted with spirits, and one day they whispered to him that he could fly if he wanted to. Of course, he wanted to. So they told him how to make wings out of feathers and he followed their instructions. Then he went up to the top of the temple of Apollo and jumped off flapping his wings. And the spirits were right. He did fly… at least for a short while until he hit the ground with a splat.

KING LEAR

And that was the end of King Bladud. His son Leir (Lear) was crowned the 10th King of the Britons and this is the King Lear that Shakespeare immortalized in his play.

The story of Prince Bladud is part of Bath's folklore and you can see several references to him around the city.

Where to see Bladud in Bath:

- **Roman Bath Statue** – A statue of King Bladud sits in an alcove just above the King's Bath in the Roman Baths.
- **Gorgon** – In the Roman Baths museum you can see a round sculpture with a man's face in the middle surrounded by his flowing hair and beard. It's called a gorgon, but he's not your typical gorgon. Gorgons are usually women who have snakes for hair. This one is male and has wings coming out of his head. Could this be a reference to flying King Bladud?
- **Prince Bladud and his Pig Statue** – In Parade Gardens you can see a Bladud statue from 1859. The pig was added in 2009.
- **The Circus** – The Circus is a historic group of Georgian townhouses designed by John Wood, the Elder between 1754 and 1768. The acorn finials on top are a nod to the favorite food of Bladud's pigs.

KING ARTHUR

HIS TOMB IS DISCOVERED IN GLASTONBURY

One of the most famous British Kings was King Arthur. Nearly everyone has heard tell of the sword he pulled from the stone, the daring deeds of his Knights of the Round Table, and his glorious court at Camelot. The stories are numerous, but there's actually little to no historic proof of an early British king called Arthur. Modern historians dismiss him as a myth, but in 1191 the monks at Glastonbury Abbey claimed they had found his tomb.

WELSH WARRIOR TO MEDIEVAL MYTH

The legendary King Arthur supposedly ruled sometime around the late 5th or early 6th century and fought against the invading Saxons. However, the first mention of a warrior called Arthur comes between 300 and 400 years later when, in 829, a Welsh monk described him as a commander who fought alongside the kings of the Britons.

Then in 1138 Geoffrey of Monmouth included King Arthur in his *History of Kings of Britain*—and the imaginative medieval storytellers took it from there. They began circulating fantastic tales of King Arthur and his daring deeds—deeds which grew more daring with each new story.

ARTHUR'S DEATH

According to Geoffrey's original story, when Arthur was seriously wounded in battle, he was put in a boat and taken to the Isle of Avalon in hopes that he could be healed. And Geoffrey ended the tale there in Avalon. But where was that mysterious Isle of Avalon? At the time, no one knew.

Fast forward to Glastonbury Abbey, 46 years after Geoffrey of Monmouth wrote Arthur's story...

FIRE DESTROYS OLD CHURCH AND RELICS

In 1184 the monks of Glastonbury Abbey were in a tizzy. Their monastery, and more importantly their Old Church had been destroyed in a fire. It wasn't just any church. It was called the Old Church because it was considered to be the first Christian church in Britain, possibly dating from the first few centuries AD.

The original structure was probably made of wattle, but it had been lovingly protected by an outer covering of wood and lead. The building itself was considered holy, but it was also chock-a-block with sacred relics that had accumulated through the years: Bones of saints, pieces of their clothing, splinters of the cross, etc. And they were all displayed in boxes made of precious metals and adorned with jewels. The church was described in the 1120s as containing "relics and reliquaries too numerous to count."

PILGRIMAGE PROBLEM

The Old Church and its hallowed objects were a big draw for pilgrims who would come to pray at the holy building and revere the relics inside. Glastonbury was one of the oldest and holiest pilgrimage sites and the donations the visitors brought made it one of the wealthiest too. So, when the monks saw the church and all their precious relics destroyed under a pile of molten lead, they knew they had a big problem. Buildings could be rebuilt, but the loss of so many sacred objects was a disaster.

With pilgrims no longer bringing in money, King Henry II stepped in with funds to help get the Abbey up and running again. The first priority was to rebuild on the holy site of the Old Church. It was decided that the Lady's Chapel would be built there, and it was completed in two years. But when King Henry died, the funding ran out and work on the rest of the Abbey slowed to a snail's pace.

FINDING A GRAVE

Then one day in 1191, seven years after the fire, the monks found the answer to their prayers (and money problems) while burying one of their own in the old Abbey cemetery. They were digging between two old stone pyramids covered in worn, unreadable markings, when deep in the ground, they found something strange.

About six or seven feet deep, they came to a large flat stone. They lifted it out and found a lead cross attached to the side that had been facing downward. They pried the cross from the stone and found an inscription hidden on the back of it. All the monks were wondering at this strange sight. Then one of them began to translate: "Here lies buried the renowned King Arthur, with Guinevere his second wife, in the isle of Avalon." Everyone gasped.

THE COFFIN

Years earlier the monks had heard a story about King Arthur being buried at Glastonbury. It was King Henry II who had sent them word. He said an old soothsayer had told him that Arthur was buried in the ancient cemetery: deep in the earth in a log casket. They had searched the Abbey grounds at the time but had found nothing. Now this seemed like a miracle that had come at just the right time: King Arthur's bones would certainly bring back the pilgrims and their sorely needed offerings.

The monks picked up their shovels and began digging again with renewed energy. They dug deeper and deeper until, at about sixteen feet, they hit what seemed to be a tree buried horizontally. It turned out to be a large tree-trunk coffin like those used in earlier times.

Word spread and a large crowd gathered (and probably paid) to see the coffin opened. After the monks had dug all around it, they struggled to lift the top off. As they hoisted the wooden lid out of the pit, the remains of two bodies were revealed: A man and a woman. There was also a lock of braided blond hair that looked completely intact—however, when a monk went to pick it up, it turned to dust in his hand.

ARTHUR'S BONES

Everyone was astonished when they saw King Arthur's skeleton: It was enormous. One monk took the shin bone and held it up against the tallest man there, and it extended a good three inches above his knee. The eye sockets were a hand's width apart, and there were at least ten wounds on his large skull. All had been scarred over except for one large one which had probably been the final fatal blow.

The monks carefully lifted the bones out of the grave and wrapped them in cloth. They would have a new marble tomb made for Arthur and Guinevere in the church. The discovery of King Arthur's grave changed Glastonbury Abbey's fortunes, as people from far and wide began making pilgrimages to see the new tomb.

OTHER KINGS

Arthur wasn't the only king laid to rest at Glastonbury. Three early Saxon Kings were buried there: Edmund I in 946, Edgar I in 975, and Edmund Ironside in 1016. As the resting place of ancient kings, Glastonbury held special meaning for the medieval monarchs who liked to fancy themselves as descendants of the courageous and chivalrous King Arthur.

Glastonbury Abbey's restoration was finally completed in 1278 (87 years after the grave had been found), and King Edward I and his wife, Queen Eleanor, paid a visit. In a special ceremony the King and Queen reverently transferred Arthur and Guinevere's bones to the new marble tomb which had been built for them and placed before the high altar. But not all their bones—their skulls and knee joints were kept out and displayed "for the people's devotion."

For the next 348 years, pilgrims flocked to Glastonbury to see King Arthur's tomb, until in 1539 the abbey faced another devastating blow: Henry VIII broke with the Catholic church, then he stripped monasteries of their wealth and tore them down. Glastonbury Abbey was left in ruins and King Arthur's tomb was lost forever.

The remains of the abbey can be visited today and the place where King Arthur's tomb once stood is marked by a sign. Historians tell us that King Arthur probably didn't exist, and that the grave discovery was most likely a hoax. But people today are just as intrigued by the mythical king as they were in the Middle Ages and even though the abbey is in ruins, they still come to look for Arthur.

KING ARTHUR'S ROUND TABLE
OR IS IT GUINEVERE'S?

*A*bout 90 miles east of King Arthur's Glastonbury grave site, you can see his Round Table. Well, sort of...

Hanging in the Great Hall in Winchester, there's a huge, old round tabletop. It brings to mind King Arthur's Round Table, and for many years, people thought it might have actually been his. Unfortunately, it's not. But let's talk about Arthur's famous Round Table first, then we'll get to the Winchester one.

ARTHUR AND GUINEVERE'S ROUND TABLE

According to medieval tales, Arthur would discuss important matters with his chivalrous knights while sitting around a large circular table. Today, such a table is seen to be a symbol of equality: Everyone sitting around it has an equally important position. We think what a clever man Arthur must have been to come up with that idea. But maybe it wasn't Arthur's idea at all and maybe it wasn't to show the ideal of equality either...

One legend seems to indicate that Arthur acquired the Round Table thanks to his wife, Guinevere. Merlin supposedly created the table for Uther Pendragon (Arthur's father), but after Uther's death the table passed to another local king called Leodegran, who just happened to be Guinevere's daddy. When Arthur and Guinevere married, the table was given to Arthur as part of his new wife's dowry.

IT'S TOO BIG

Now, I can't say for sure, but I think the newlyweds probably didn't know what to do with that big unwieldy table. It was too big for the breakfast room and they already had a perfectly good dining table, so they shoved it up in the attic and went about their royal business.

As Arthur's reputation for being a righteous ruler spread throughout Europe, princes and rulers came from everywhere to sit in his court and learn from him. He became a mentor and inspiration to many men of valor.

However, in those days, social rank was a mighty big deal, and at gatherings everyone expected to be seated according to their status. When men showed up with the same titles, they would fight over which one got the seat closest to the head of the table. This gave Arthur a lot of headaches.

One day he came home complaining *again* about his knights. "They're never happy. I told them it didn't matter where they sat, that everyone would have equal input. But fights broke out because those with the higher ranks still wanted to sit at the head of the table. I finally had to stop it when swords were drawn.

"So I decided to put all the names in a hat and draw them randomly for each seat. But they weren't happy with that either. The ones who thought they were being slighted sulked through the whole meeting and wouldn't participate. Honestly, they are worse than children."

GUINEVERE HAS THE ANSWER

Guinevere looked up from her embroidery and smiled up at him. "Darling, we already have the perfect solution to your problem. It's up in the attic. Remember that big round table from my father? If you use that, there'll be no head of the table for them to fight over. Then maybe you can get something done."

Arthur hit his forehead with the palm of his hand. "Why didn't I think of that? Sweetheart, you're a genius."

That night Arthur slept better than he had in a good long while. The next day he ordered the big table moved into the meeting room. And when his knights came in, they couldn't figure out which seat was the most important, so they just sat down and got to work.

So maybe we have to rethink Arthur's cleverness and give the credit to Guinevere. And maybe the Round Table wasn't brought out because of high ideals of equality, but just to stop the constant squabbling about who got to sit where.

THE WINCHESTER ROUND TABLE

If you want to get an idea of what Arthur's (and Guinevere's) table might have been like, have a look at the Winchester Round Table. The painted wooden tabletop hangs in the Great Hall which is all that remains of Winchester Castle. It's 18 feet in diameter and weighs over a ton. It was once supported by twelve sturdy legs, and it has been hanging in this hall for at least the last 500 years—maybe more.

At one time, people believed it was actually King Arthur's Round Table. But alas, Arthur never put his elbows up on this table. In 1976 it was taken down for radiocarbon dating, and the tests showed that the timber was cut between 1250 and 1280: So it's a medieval construction made at least 600 years after King Arthur was supposed to have lived. But it's still pretty impressive and historic.

The first written record we have of the Winchester Round Table hanging in this hall is in 1464, when John Hardyng wrote:

> "The Rounde Table at Wynchestere beganne,
> and ther it ende, and ther it hangeth yet."

This was written during the time that the table was considered to be King Arthur's and Winchester was associated with Camelot—possibly because of the table.

REAL KINGS AND ROUND TABLES

Medieval people were obsessed with King Arthur, and tales of his exploits were all the rage. Kings fancied themselves as continuing in the mighty ruler's footsteps, and their faithful knights dreamed of sitting at the Round Table recounting their chivalrous deeds.

One way that kings could recreate Arthurian times was to sponsor a Round Table Tournament. I imagine they were similar to our medieval festivals of today. There was jousting, feasting, dancing, etc. Everyone pretended to be Arthurian: Chivalrous, courteous, and righteous.

EDWARD I

One royal Arthurian fan was King Edward I. He was thrilled when the monks of Glastonbury Abbey found Arthur and Guinevere's grave. And he participated in the ceremony to place their bones in the new tomb in the cathedral.

He also hosted Round Table Tournaments. One was held in 1290 near Winchester to celebrate the betrothals of his children. Historians think the Winchester Round Table was probably made for that occasion. Then after the festival, they had to find a place to store that big table, so they hung it in the Great Hall in Winchester Castle where it remains to this day.

HENRY VIII

About 200 years after Edward I had the Round Table made for his tournament, Henry VIII came on the scene. He was another king who felt closely connected to Arthur. He visited Winchester Castle and saw the table in 1516. He decided it would be a good thing to show off to the Holy Roman Emperor, Charles V, when he came for a state visit.

So Henry had the table painted in the design we see today. In the process, he made sure that the connection between Arthur's reign and his own was clear. In the center of the table is Henry's emblem, the Tudor rose. At the top is a likeness of King Arthur. But since no one knew what Arthur looked like, Henry decided his own likeness would do just fine. So what we see today is King Arthur with a young Henry Tudor's face.

Even though the huge Round Table hanging in Winchester's Great Hall didn't belong to King Arthur, it's a good representation of what medieval people thought Arthur's table looked like. For years people believed it *was* Arthur's table, and by association, it may have soaked up some of the mystique and magic associated with those fabulous Arthurian tales.

BOUDICA

QUEEN, MOTHER, WARRIOR, AND FOLK HERO

*N*ow that we've talked about a few kings of questionable existence, let's move on to a very real queen.

In central London, at the end of Westminster Bridge, just across from Big Ben, stands a sculpture of a woman driving a chariot. She has two young girls with her, and she looks fierce. The statue is called *Boadicea and Her Daughters*. As an American I had never heard of this woman, and I was curious.

QUEEN BOUDICA

As it turns out, Boudica was an early British Queen turned folk hero that all British children learn about in school. Nowadays her name is spelled Boudica (pronounced something like Boo' di-ka) instead of Boadicea, and her claim to fame is that she took on the Roman army—and *almost* won.

But before the tall, red-headed Queen set out in her chariot to wreak havoc on the Romans, she probably wasn't so fierce. Her life was probably pretty good. She was married to Prasutagus, King of the Iceni tribe, and they had two young daughters.

The Iceni were a small Celtic tribe, from eastern Britain—in and around present-day Norfolk. They were independent and wealthy, and they were a *client kingdom* of Rome. That meant they were subject to the great Empire but still maintained a certain amount of self-rule. It also meant that they received some financial support from Rome. Everything was coming up roses for Queen Boudica until 60 AD. That's when her husband died.

THE KING IS DEAD

Prasutagus left a will giving half his kingdom to his daughters and the other half to Rome. Queen Boudica would govern for the girls until they were of age. The royal couple must have thought this 50/50 arrangement would ensure Rome's continued support and protection. But they were wrong.

While the Iceni people had no problem with a female ruler, the Romans did. According to Roman law, a girl could not inherit from her father and a woman certainly could not reign over men.

There was another problem too—a financial one. Back in Rome, Nero was burning through money like crazy and looking for ways to replenish his coffers. He declared that all the funds given to the *client kingdoms* in Britain had been loans and he was calling them all in.

Rome declared that since the agreement for protection and funding had been with King Prasutagus, and since he had died without male heirs, everything belonged to Rome. And they came to collect.

Roman soldiers rode in and plundered the settlement. Queen Boudica protested, but they stripped her, tied her to a post, and beat her. Then they raped her two young daughters. Boudica was devastated... and angry... very, very angry. And everyone knows you don't want to make a redhead mad. She vowed that she would have revenge.

REVENGE

While the governor of Britain, Suetonius, was away in the west attacking the Druids, Boudica set her plan into action. She rallied other local tribes and gathered an army. Many of the tribes were disillusioned with Roman rule and happy to join Queen Boudica. Her army numbered into the tens of thousands.

The furious Queen led her army to Colchester, the capital of Roman Britain, then to London, and finally to St. Albans. In each city, they killed the inhabitants, looted, and burned what remained. Modern-day archaeologists have found a layer of burned earth in each area, which they call the *Boudiccan destruction horizon*.

Boudica's rampage had killed about 70,000 Romans and Roman sympathizers. Her army also ambushed Roman troops and killed about 1,500 soldiers. She was making Governor Suetonius look bad on the reports going back to Rome. He had to do something.

THE SHOWDOWN

Boudica's army had been very successful using guerrilla tactics. But now Suetonius would force them to face the Roman army head-on. He assembled his troops in a valley with a woodland at their back. The Britons faced them and used their wagons behind them to block retreat. There was no getting out of it. It was a fight to the death.

Boudica had between 100,000 and 200,000 on her side and the Romans numbered about 10,000. As they prepared to fight, each commander was giving a pep talk to their troops. Boudica was in her chariot with her two daughters riding up and down the line of soldiers shouting that they had right on their side and the gods were with them.

As was their tradition, the Britons had painted themselves blue, using a mixture made from the woad plant. This gave them a fearsome look and was also a sort of camouflage in twilight hours.

The Britons knew how to fight one on one, but the Roman army was more like a machine. They marched in impenetrable formations, clad in protective metal armor. And they slaughtered Queen Boudica's army. Boudica herself survived the battle, but one account says she took poison rather than be captured, and another version says she died of disease shortly afterward.

BOUDICA LIVES ON

Boudica's revenge was fierce, but in the end, it failed. The Romans went on to rule Britain for another 400 years. However, Queen Boudica's courage was not forgotten, and she was an inspiration to future queens. In the sixteenth century, Elizabeth I used Boudica's story as an example to prove that a woman was fit to be queen on her own. Then in the 1800s, during Victoria's reign, Prince Albert revived the tale of Boudica's strength as a tribute to his wife. She was seen as Boudica's namesake because the names Boudica and Victoria both meant Victory.

The Warrior Queen's name has been written many ways throughout the centuries: Boadicea, Boudicea, Boudicca... But no matter how her name is spelled, she has remained in the hearts of the British people as a symbol of the fearlessness and independence of the British spirit.

BRITISH ROYALS AND SWANS

IT'S ILLEGAL TO EAT THE QUEEN'S SWANS

The British Monarchy owns lots of things: They possess homes, palaces, and castles all over the country. But did you know they also own most of the swans in the UK? British kings and queens have enjoyed a long relationship with the regal white bird.

At one time, anyone could own a few swans. Then in 1482 the king decreed that those owning less than a certain amount of land had to forfeit their long-necked birds. And who were they forfeited to? The king, of course. The law went on to set out prison sentences and fines for anyone caught trying to catch or kill a swan or interfere with their breeding or nesting. Common people could no longer own, hunt, or eat swans.

DO YOU HAVE A SWAN LICENSE?

Having elegant white birds swimming around in your lake or castle moat became a status symbol. So, of course, all the aristocrats just had to have them. The monarchy found a way to cash in on this fad too. You had to register for a "brand" which would be carved into the swan's bill, and make sure your birds' wings were clipped. Because any unmarked swans on open water became the property of the king. And that's still the law today.

Even so, lots of lords wanted swans, and between 1450 and 1600 there were about 630 brands recorded for London waters. As time passed, swans went out of fashion, and many lost interest and let their license lapse. Today, only two organizations (other than the monarchy) still hold the right to have swans on the Thames River: The Vintners Company and the Worshipful Company of Dyers—both ancient guilds who have held this privilege for hundreds of years.

BRANDS

The brands, or hieroglyphic-type markings, were carved into the birds' bills until the early twentieth century. Queen Alexandra took pity on her winged subjects and requested that the markings be simplified and less damaging to the swans. Later, the monarchy stopped marking their birds altogether—since all unmarked swans belonged to them anyway.

The Dyers' streamlined their mark into a single nick on one side of the bill and the Vintners put a nick on each side. This is the origin of the pub name "A Swan with Two Necks"— it's a corruption of "a swan with two nicks."

SWAN ON THE TABLE

Why were the king and his aristocratic friends so interested in swans? Well, it wasn't only for their graceful beauty—they also liked gobbling them up for Christmas dinner. Often the carcass (feathers and all) was used as a decorative centerpiece on the table, or as an elaborate topping for a swan pie.

But people didn't eat just any old swan: Mature birds are very tough, so it was the young that were destined for the dinner table. They were selected in July, placed in a fenced-off pond, and fattened up on grain.

As we all know from Hans Christian Andersen's "Ugly Duckling," young swans are greyish until they mature and get their white feathers. When these feathers start to come in, they are at their most succulent. And, as it happens, young swans hatch in spring and start to get their white feathers just about Christmas time. That's perfect timing for hungry aristocrats—not so good for swans.

UPPING THE SWANS

So, if you are a ravenous royal looking forward to roast swan and swan pie for Christmas, how do you go about finding those young birds to fatten up? You have a "swan upping." The upping is the annual swan count on the River Thames—a tradition that goes back 900 years.

Originally these uppings were to declare ownership of the young swans by giving them the same mark as their parents —and to select those who would end up on the dinner table. Even though swans are no longer eaten in the UK, the young are still marked as belonging to either the Monarchy, the Dyers, or the Vintners.

The traditional upping is still carried out today, but the process has been updated. Instead of having notches carved into their bills, the swans on the Thames are now tagged with a leg band. These bands are linked to a database which is used to monitor the health and numbers of the swan population. The Vintner and Dyers add a second leg band to their birds to identify their ownership.

The upping takes place in the third week of July and lasts five days. Three teams representing the Monarchy, the Dyers, and the Vintners wear their respective upping uniforms and display their corresponding flags. The upping starts with a toast to the Seigneur of the Swans, which is one of the lesser-known titles of the British monarch.

When they spot a family of swans, they cry, "All-Up!" and surround the birds with their boats. Each cob (male), pen (female), and cygnet (youngster) is lifted out of the water. The cygnets get their new identity leg band, and everyone gets a thorough health check. The upping has also become an opportunity to educate children about swans, and school activities are often planned around it. The swan upping is a great example of an old tradition that has adapted with the times.

ROYAL ASCOT AND HORSE RACING
THANKS TO QUEEN ANNE

*W*hen you find yourself in the train station surrounded by lots of women wearing fancy hats and men dressed in tails and top hats, it can mean only one thing: It's time for the Royal Ascot horse races.

Royal Ascot is the most important horse racing event in the UK. It's held every year over five days in June at the Ascot racecourse near Windsor Castle. The Royals love it and attend regularly. Queen Elizabeth usually arrives at 2:00 pm riding along part of the track in her horse-drawn carriage before the race begins.

QUEEN ANNE

This famous race has been associated with the Royals since 1711 when it was first introduced by Queen Anne. The story goes that one day she was taking a ride, surveying her kingdom around Windsor Castle when she came upon a nice flat stretch of land. She thought it looked just perfect for horse racing, and she set up the first race with a prize of 100 guineas.

Queen Anne knew it would be difficult to keep the crowds off the track, so she put her guards in charge of royal protection and crowd control. Their official title was Yeomen Prickers because they were armed with sharp pikes that they used to prick people and clear them off the racetrack. Today they no longer prick and poke people with sharp sticks, so their title has been changed to Greencoats because of the green velvet suits they wear.

One legend says they wear green suits because Queen Anne had ordered lots of green velvet to have curtains made for Windsor Castle. After all the castle windows had been covered, a lot of fabulous fabric remained. And being a thrifty monarch, Queen Anne decided to use the left-over cloth to have sumptuous suits made for her Yeomen Prickers.

We don't have any record telling us what Queen Anne wore to that first race, but we can imagine she was royally decked-out. And wearing your Sunday best to the races is a practice that continues to this day. In fact, Royal Ascot seems to be just as much about fashion as it is about racing. And the ladies' hats steal the show. There's more news coverage about who *wore* what than who *won* what. Going to the races is a beloved British tradition and everyone is expected to dress the part. The dress code (and hat code) varies depending on your seating area, but everyone is encouraged to dress up.

If you can't make it to Royal Ascot, don't worry, there are plenty of smaller races and other events at Ascot throughout the year. It's a fun day out and a chance to show off your best hat.

GUY FAWKES AND BONFIRE NIGHT
THANKS TO KING JAMES I

When we moved to London in the summer of 2003, we were coming from an America still in shock from the September 11 bombings. So when November rolled around and I started hearing booming noises in the night, I was a bit jittery.

As it turned out, it was just the fireworks used in the celebration of Bonfire Night, also known as Guy Fawkes Night, a British tradition that goes back more than 400 years. Of course, I wanted to know the whole story...

A GUY CALLED GUY

In 1605 Guy Fawkes tried to blow up the King and Parliament. He didn't succeed, but he did earn a degree of fame for himself. Even if his name is unfamiliar to some of us, we will recognize his face from the masks of the Anonymous movement.

"Remember, remember the fifth of November
The gunpowder treason and plot.
I see no reason why gunpowder treason
Should ever be forgot."

It seems the whole kerfuffle started when King James I decided to persecute those who didn't share his religious beliefs. James I became King of England in 1603 and, being Protestant, he passed laws that made life very difficult for Catholics. His subjects were "strongly encouraged" to convert to the religion of their monarch.

A few years later, a small group of Catholics who were tired of the King's persecution decided to take matters into their own hands. They made a plan to blow up Parliament and the King along with it, setting the date for 5 November 1605. It was the opening session of Parliament and the King would be present.

They recruited a soldier called Guy Fawkes who was born in England but had been fighting in the Spanish army for several years and had a knowledge of explosives. The group of conspirators rented a house close to Parliament and started digging a tunnel as a way to get the explosives into the building. But they had a bit of luck when a cellar located under the Parliament building came up for rent. And even better, the cellar was directly under the King's throne.

They put down their shovels and rented the cellar. Then they filled it with 36 barrels of gunpowder. They stacked firewood on top of, and around, the explosive powder kegs to hide them. Apparently, it was common practice to rent out the cellars under Parliament, and firewood was often stored there.

"Guy Fawkes, 'twas his intent
To blow up King and Parliament.
Three score barrels were laid below
To prove old England's overthrow."

One of the conspirators sent an anonymous letter to Lord Monteagle advising him not to attend the opening of parliament. It said something terrible was going to happen. Not knowing what to make of this warning, Lord Monteagle showed it to the others. They decided that it must surely be a hoax. But just as a precaution, the cellars were searched the day before the opening ceremony.

Guy was there, dressed as a servant, with his innocent bundles of firewood, and the guards didn't seem suspicious. But later that night they came back for a second check and found Guy there again. This time he was dressed in his traveling clothes (and apparently holding a dark lantern and lighted match). They questioned him, searched the cellar, and found the gunpowder.

Guy was arrested and tortured until he gave the names of the other plotters. The seven ringleaders were tried and executed. They were hung, drawn and quartered, and their remains were sent to the four corners of the kingdom as a warning to any others who might be hatching a similar plot.

"By God's mercy he was catch'd
With a dark lantern and lighted match
Holler boys, holler boys, let the bells ring
Holler boys, holler boys, God save the King!"

BONFIRE NIGHT

To celebrate the King's deliverance, the people lit bonfires. And they've done the same every fifth of November for over 400 years. Of course, the festivity has evolved in that time: At some point it was decided that Guy's original punishment wasn't good enough and that he should be burned on the bonfire every year. So the tradition of burning "Guys" became part of the festivities.

These "Guy" effigies were made by stuffing old clothes with paper and then adding a Guy Fawkes mask to the head as a final touch. In bygone days, the children were in charge of preparations for bonfire night and it was up to them to make the "Guy." When they finished they would parade him through the neighborhood in a wagon or pram, or carry him in a chair and ask for "a penny for the Guy." Today, the "Guys" are less popular than they once were.

JUST A REGULAR GUY

In fact, this is how the word "guy," that we now use for a man whose name we don't know, came into common use. At first "guy" meant a man who was funny looking and, usually, badly dressed – like the Guys that the children made. To call someone a guy was not a compliment. But over the years the word lost its negative meaning and now it can be used for anyone, whether they are funny looking or not.

The reputation of Guy Fawkes has improved over the years as well. After a book that presented him in a sympathetic manner came out in 1841, he became a character in children's stories and comic books. In 1985 a comic book called *V for Vendetta* was created which inspired a 2005 film by the same name. The main character "V" has many parallels with Guy Fawkes and he wears a Guy Fawkes mask as he tries to overthrow a future UK government that has lost touch with the people, and taken away their freedom.

THE MASK

The Guy Fawkes mask worn in the film was adopted by several groups, such as Anonymous and the Occupy Movement, to allow them to protest in anonymity. It can now be seen at protests around the world. Some countries such as Bahrain and Saudi Arabia have even banned its importation, calling it "a symbol of rebels and revenge." But that hasn't decreased its popularity, as is seen by the fact that it is one of the top sellers on Amazon.

The story of Guy Fawkes and the celebrations of bonfire night are meant to remind us of the dangers of threatening the government. But it seems that Guy's story has taken on a new meaning and he has now become a symbol of protest against causes perceived as unjust. I can't help but think the original Guy would be pleased that his image is being used in this way.

- *A little disclaimer: I'm all for peaceful protests, I think they're healthy for society. But I'm completely against all forms of violence.*

GOD SAVE THE ROYAL DERRIERE
THE BRITISH NATIONAL ANTHEM MIGHT HAVE BEEN FRENCH (OH MY!)

*T*he British National Anthem, "God Save the Queen" (or King, depending on the gender of the monarch), is played at all royal events, but did you ever wonder about its origins? It seems this song could be yet another link in the intertwined histories of the United Kingdom and France. According to some, this song was written in France during the time when Louis XIV was facing a difficult and dangerous surgery...

In 1686, the King began to have pain in a very delicate area. All the best doctors were called to Versailles to investigate the King's *derrière*. He was diagnosed with a *fistule anale* (anal fistula) which was possibly caused by too much horseback riding. The doctors tried everything they could think of, but, alas, the King's bottom still hurt. As a last resort, they called in Charles-Francois Felix de Tassy, the barber/surgeon. In the 17th century, doctors didn't operate on people—that was the domain of the barbers. Barbers performed small surgeries, such as tooth extraction and bloodletting, in between their shaves and haircuts.

BRING IN THE BARBER

Felix the Barber carefully studied the King's painful posterior. As you can imagine, he wasn't too keen to start cutting on the royal bottom. If it didn't go well, the consequences would be serious—for the King, the country, and for Felix himself. This type of surgery had never been done before, but poor sweating Felix realized there was no other option.

He asked the King to give him six months to practice and figure out exactly what to do. He would also need people to practice on, so he would need to "borrow" men from hospitals and prisons who had the same condition. The King kindly granted Felix's request.

Felix was delving into uncharted territory. Not only did he have to figure out how to correct the King's problem, he also had to design and make the tools necessary to perform the operation. And all along the way, he tested his new tools and techniques on the King's loyal subjects.

He performed the operation on 75 men—some of them even survived. And those who didn't were buried in the wee hours of the morning so as not to alarm the public about the King's chances of survival.

FELIX IS READY

When the barber was fairly confident that he could perform the surgery without killing the King, the operation was scheduled. A nervous Felix did the deed—a three-hour surgery, without anesthesia. Felix's months of practice paid off and the King was up and around in no time.

Since everyone at court wanted to copy the king, it soon became quite fashionable to have an anal fistula. There were many requests for the same surgery, but Felix's days of cutting bottoms were over. After performing the King's operation, he hung up his surgical instruments—which, by the way, can be seen today in the Museum of the History of Medicine in Paris. The grateful King Louis rewarded Felix with lands, money, and a title, so I don't imagine he needed to give haircuts any longer either.

BUT WHAT ABOUT THE SONG?

Even though the Palace tried to keep it quiet, word leaked out about the King's condition, his impending surgery, and the "practice patients" who didn't make it. All over France, Louis XIV's loyal subjects were praying for their King's survival. At the Royal Girls School in St-Cyr, a few miles from Versailles, Madame de Brinon, the headmistress, wrote the words to "God Save the King." It was a prayer asking God to protect the King during his surgery, and the girls of the school recited it every day.

After Louis had recovered, he scheduled a visit to the school. Madame de Brinon had Jean-Baptiste Lully set the words to music and the girls sang it when the King arrived. It became a tradition that each time the King would visit, the girls would greet him with the song, "God Save the King."

SWIPED BY HANDEL

The composer Handel, who was living in London, passed through Paris in 1714 and heard the song. He took it back to the UK, had it translated into English, and eventually it became the national anthem that is now played at all events where the royal family is present.

So it seems that the British national anthem might have originally been a song asking God to look after the King of France during his bum surgery. But Madame de Brinon was a discreet woman, and in her song she never mentioned exactly what the King needed saving from. Therefore, the song ended up as a generic prayer that was suitable for many situations. So next time you hear "God Save the Queen," try not to think of Louis XIV's painful bottom.

GOD SAVE ALL THE KINGS AND QUEENS

The British weren't the only people to borrow this song. It has been used at various times by Prussia/Germany, Russia, Switzerland, Denmark, Hawaii, Sweden, and Iceland. As their monarchies disappeared, so did the song (so maybe it wasn't all that effective). It's still used in Norway and Liechtenstein and in many of the Commonwealth countries.

The music is also the tune used for the American patriotic song, "My Country, 'Tis of Thee."

The above story, explaining the origins of the lyrics to "God Save the King/Queen," comes from *Souvenirs de la Marquise de Créquy de 1710 à 1803.* The truthfulness of this account has been called into question and there are many theories about where the music and lyrics originated—but I rather like this version.

VI

THIS AND THAT

A MIXED BAG OF BRITISH CULTURE

Language
Attitude
Health Care
Taxes
and a Saint

DIVIDED BY A COMMON LANGUAGE
AMERICAN ENGLISH VS BRITISH ENGLISH

*W*hen we moved to England from America, I didn't expect any problems with the language. After all, English was my mother tongue. What a surprise then, when I found out that British English and American English could be very different.

I would often run into words that had one meaning in the UK and a different meaning in the US. And one area where this was most apparent (and embarrassing) was clothing.

CLOTHING

As we talk of clothing, let's begin with those problematic undergarments: Americans visiting Britain often mention their underwear without meaning to because they just don't know the vocabulary...

Americans wear underpants under their pants while Brits wear *pants* under their *trousers*. It can be embarrassing for an American to mention that they bought their new pants on sale and then to realize that people think they're talking about their underwear.

Clothing

Pants

Vest

Suspenders

Braces

An American wears an undershirt under his shirt to keep him warm, while a Brit wears a *vest* under his shirt for added warmth.

An American prefers to wear his *vest* over his shirt to look *sharp*, but a Brit might wear a waistcoat over his shirt to look *smart*.

An American woman might wear *garters* to hold up her stockings, but a British woman would use *suspenders*.

American men wear *suspenders* to hold up their *pants* but British men wear *braces* to hold up their *trousers*.

Americans put *braces* on their teeth to straighten them and Brits do too, but hopefully not the same ones that hold up their trousers.

An American baby wears *diapers* and has a *pacifier* in his mouth, but a British baby wears *nappies* and has a *dummy* in his mouth.

AROUND THE HOUSE

Even around the house there can be communication problems. In one of the apartments (flats) we lived in, there was a leak in the kitchen, so I called the landlord to report that water was leaking around the *faucet*.

-Where's the leak?
- Just around the bottom of the faucet.
- (Pause) ...And where is the faucet?
- (Pause) ...Umm, it's on the sink (where else would a faucet be?)
- (Pause) ...Ohhh! You must mean the tap.
- Well... yes, I guess so.

An American gets water from the *faucet*, stores food in a *cabinet*, and cooks it on a *burner* on top of the *stove*.

A Brit gets water from the *tap*, stores food in a *cupboard*, and cooks on a *hob* on the top of the *cooker*.

An American enters a building on the *first floor* and walks upstairs to the *second floor*—unless, of course, he's really *tired*—then he takes the *elevator*.

A Brit enters on the *ground floor* and walks upstairs to the *first floor*—unless he is really *knackered*—then he takes the *lift*.

An American might go into the *living room*, sit on the *sofa* and watch the *TV* which is plugged into an *electrical outlet*.

A Brit goes into the *lounge*, sits on the *settee* and watches the *telly* which is connected to a *power point*.

AUTOMOBILES AND MOTOR CARS

Yes, cars are different too:

An American might drive a four-door *sedan* that has a *hood* at the front, a *trunk* at the back, and runs on *gas*.

A Brit drives a *saloon* with a *bonnet* at the front, a *boot* at the back, and runs on *petrol*.

BATH ROOM, REST ROOM, OR TOILET?

Another thing that can cause misunderstandings between Americans and Brits is bathroom and toilet vocabulary.

Americans might use the word *bathroom* or *restroom* for any room in which they can relieve themselves. A room with a toilet and sink might be called a *powder room* (where ladies go to powder their noses).

In the UK a *bathroom* is a room where you can take a bath. A *toilet* is the room containing the *WC* (water closet). This room can also be called a *WC, loo,* or *lavatory*.

NEED A BATH OR A REST?

A British friend once told me of an American visitor who was speaking at a conference in the UK. He asked someone for the restroom and was taken to a lovely room which contained a sofa and nice soft chairs—the perfect place for him to have a little rest. Boy, was he confused as he looked around for the toilet! And the Brits were wondering why he needed a rest before the meeting had even begun.

CLOAKROOM OR TOILET?

Occasionally you will see the term *cloakroom* used to mean toilet but cloakroom can also be a place to hang coats (especially in hotels). When I was new to London and looking at apartments, I saw an ad that boasted of a *"guest cloakroom."* I wondered what it could be. Was it a closet for coats? Would that really be a special feature to mention in an ad? After pondering it for a bit, I realized in all the flats I'd looked at, I hadn't actually seen any with coat closets, so maybe it was something special.

Soon after, while looking at a different flat I heard the estate agent, who was around the corner, say "Oh, and there's a guest cloakroom." So I hurried in the direction of her voice and found her in a hallway where there were two closed doors. I had a 50/50 chance. I opened one and saw that it was, in fact, a closet and said, "Yes, a guest cloakroom." The estate agent looked a bit surprised, opened the other door revealing a toilet and said, "No, this is the guest cloakroom." …It looked like a restroom to me.

Spend a Penny: A Brit who's going to the loo might say he's going to "spend a penny." This phrase goes back to the 1850s when public toilets were fitted with locks which cost a penny to open.

ERASER OR CONDOM?

In the US the rubber piece on the end of a pencil which is used to erase mistakes is called an *eraser*. In the UK it's called a *rubber*. But in the US, a rubber means a condom. You can see how this might be confusing.

Here is a funny story about a Brit who had a young daughter who collected novelty erasers. While in the US, he went into a Christian bookstore ...

- Lady behind the counter: Good morning Sir, how may I help you?
- Mr X: Good morning, I'd like to buy some rubbers.
- Lady (blushing): Sir, we don't sell that kind of thing here. This is a Christian bookstore.
- Mr X: Oh, that's a shame. They're for my daughter. She really wanted one with the Stars and Stripes on it...
- Lady (bright red): Sir, I...
- Mr X: I also thought you might stock some rubbers with Bible verses printed on them.
- Lady: Excuse me for a second, I need to call the manager!

My husband also experienced a moment of confusion with this term. He was a newly arrived American, sitting in a class in the UK, when an attractive lady leaned over to him and whispered, "Do you have a rubber?" At first, he was taken aback (and maybe a bit flattered), but then he realized that she just wanted to borrow an eraser.

SOME INTERESTING EXPRESSIONS

Both Americans and Brits have expressions that sound a bit odd the first time you hear them. Here are a few that I found amusing or confusing:

From American to British

- I'm shocked (flabbergasted) = I'm *gobsmacked.*
- I am so happy = I'm *chuffed* (or chuffed to bits).
- That's another story = That's a different *kettle of fish.*
- Would you like a snack? = Do you fancy some *nibbles?*
- Don't get all worked up = Don't get your *knickers in a twist.*
- It's going well (hunky dorey) = It's *tickety-boo.* (A bit old-fashioned.)
- It all went wrong = It all went *pear-shaped.*
- They're as different as night and day = They're like *chalk and cheese.*
- And that's it! (usually at the end of some instructions) = *And Bob's your uncle!*

I hope these stories gave you a bit of a chuckle and maybe helped to expand your "English" vocabulary.

KEEP CALM AND CARRY ON
THE SLOGAN THAT SUMS UP
THE BRITISH SPIRIT

*W*hat could be more British than the KEEP CALM AND CARRY ON poster? I'm sure everyone has seen this catchy slogan and many variations of it. It seems to pop up everywhere: On posters, T-shirts, mugs, phone cases, and just about anything that can be printed upon. This snappy little phrase sums up that stoicism that we admire so much in the British: Their ability to take whatever life throws their way, deal with it, and keep going.

It especially calls to mind the British resolve during the continuous bombings of the Second World War for which this poster was designed. The slogan was originally intended to encourage calmness during the darkest days of war. However, it wasn't actually seen by the general public until the 21st century...

CARRYING ON DURING THE WAR

During the First World War, Britain, and especially London, experienced the first sustained bombing campaign in history. It changed the whole idea of war. No longer were there soldiers fighting at the front lines to protect their families who were safe at home, tucked out of harm's way. In this new type of war, ordinary citizens were targeted in their own homes.

As the Second World War approached, the British government knew that its citizens would once again be under attack. They wanted to find a way to reassure them and encourage them to keep up morale when things got tough.

The answer, they decided, was posters. The Ministry of Information designed a template. The message would be printed on an eye-catching red background with a message in bright white capital letters, and each poster would have the crown at the top (a symbol of the state). With this straightforward design, the posters would be easily recognizable, and they could print new messages as needed.

The committee settled on three slogans and started production in 1939 just before the declaration of war. They were:

FREEDOM IS IN PERIL,
DEFEND IT WITH ALL YOUR MIGHT

—

YOUR COURAGE, YOUR CHEERFULNESS,
YOUR RESOLUTION WILL BRING US VICTORY

—

KEEP CALM AND CARRY ON

The plan was to display these posters as needed at extremely difficult moments when morale might be low—after a major crisis or, in the worst case scenario, after a Nazi invasion.

FIRST TWO POSTERS FLOP

In September 1939 war was declared and the government had every reason to expect heavy bombing to begin within hours. They rushed to plaster the country with the first two posters: "Freedom Is In Peril, Defend It With All Your Might" and "Your Courage, Your Cheerfulness, Your Resolution Will Bring Us Victory." They saved the third poster ("Keep Calm and Carry On") for an even worse event.

To everyone's surprise (and relief) the expected bombings didn't start immediately. And for the first year or so, it was relatively quiet on the home front. The civilian population didn't seem to be in imminent danger or distress, but the country had already been papered with the first two posters. The bright red and white signs in ALL CAPS were shouting at British citizens to keep up their morale.

The people, who saw themselves as already being courageous, cheerful and resolute, viewed the posters as patronizing. With the crown at the top, they felt talked down to by an upper class who didn't know them or understand their mood. In addition, the message was too vague. What exactly were they supposed to do? Was there really nothing more to winning a war than being cheerful?

Seeing the public reaction to their first well-intentioned messages, the Ministry of Information changed their tactics. They began printing posters with images and giving advice about specific actions to take, such as grow your own food, mend instead of spend, don't waste food, etc.

LOST AND FOUND

The third, and arguably the best, poster, "Keep Calm and Carry On" never saw the light of day. It stayed stored away until 1940. Then most of them were pulped as part of the Paper Salvage Campaign. However, a few posters with the catchy saying escaped the shredder, and sixty years later, in 2000, one of them showed up in a bookstore called Barter Books in northeast England. The shop owners, Stuart and Mary Manley, had bought a box of books at auction, and in the bottom was a "Keep Calm and Carry On" poster.

They thought it was eye-catching and charming, so they framed it and hung it in their shop. Customers began to comment on it and ask where they could get one. The Manleys saw an opportunity and contacted the Ministry of Defense to see if the poster was under copyright. It wasn't, so they started printing and selling copies. Soon others snapped up the snappy slogan and began printing their own posters.

KEEP CALM AND...

Some clever people noticed that this simple saying was very versatile, and they began to make parody versions. Today you can find adaptations of this slogan printed on just about anything.

You can keep calm and: Drink beer, eat cupcakes, swim on, rock on, travel on, drink tea, love life, go shopping, curry on, play golf, eat chocolate...

In addition, this malleable motto can be used in the negative:

I can't keep calm: I'm Irish, I'm the bride, I'm an artist, the internet is down, I'm a drama queen, I'm studying history...

The bright red and white sign that admonishes us to keep calm (all the while shouting at us with its capital letters) was spurned during the war years but has been lovingly adopted and adapted in the 21st century.

Perhaps its popularity is down to its simplicity and versatility. Or it could be that its quiet resolve is fitting for our stressful, modern lives. It's still a good reminder of how to react in the face of the many pressures of daily life.

I have to say that my favorite is definitely *"Keep Calm and Eat Chocolate."*

FLORENCE NIGHTINGALE
THE LADY WITH THE LAMP AND PIE CHART

*E*ngland is rightly proud of its National Health Service. The NHS was founded in 1948 and based on the premise that healthcare should be freely available to anyone in need. But even before the NHS was thought of, there were reformers working in the field of health care.

One of them was Florence Nightingale. Most people think of her as the lamp-carrying nurse who, during the Crimean War, would check on each soldier during the night. After the war, however, she spent the rest of her life writing about how to improve patient care—and using charts to get her point across.

A GIRL NAMED FLORENCE

Florence Nightingale was named after Florence, Italy, the city of her birth. In 1817, wealthy British landowner William Nightingale married Frances Smith and soon thereafter they set out on a three-year honeymoon tour of Italy. (Yes, three years—they really knew how to honeymoon in those days!)

Frances became pregnant, but they were having so much fun they didn't have time to be thinking about baby names. So when their first daughter was born in Naples in 1819, they called her Parthenope after the Greek name of that city. Thirteen months later they were in Florence, Italy when their second daughter arrived, and, of course, they named her Florence.

The following year, the Nightingale family went back to England where Florence grew up in the family home in Hampshire. She didn't go to school, but was educated by her parents at home. She learned French, German, and Italian, and had a special fondness for mathematics.

CALLED TO BE A NURSE

Florence's parents expected her to grow up, marry, and have a family like all respectable young ladies of her day. But even as a young girl, Florence thought her life might go in a different direction. One day, as she was sitting under a tree reading, she felt God speak to her. He told her that she had a special calling to help others. At the time, Florence didn't know exactly what that meant, but she continued to have similar experiences from time to time throughout her early years.

When she was around seventeen, Florence finally realized what her calling was: She would be a nurse and help the sick. However, at the time, neither hospitals nor nurses had very good reputations. Hospitals were dirty places where people died. Nurses were crude, rough women who drank a lot and showed little compassion to their patients. Respectable women did not become nurses, and Florence's parents forbade it. They encouraged her to find a nice suitable man, marry, have children, and forget all about that nursing nonsense.

TROUBLES AT HOME

For the next decade or so, the Nightingale household was in turmoil. Florence kept insisting she was called to be a nurse, and her parents kept refusing and trying to find a man for her to marry. Florence, now nearly thirty years old, was close to a breakdown from the conflict.

Her parents decided a change of scenery might get all those crazy nursing ideas out of her head. So they sent her on a European holiday with family friends. But while the others were sightseeing or wandering through museums, Florence was doing research. She visited hospitals in France, Italy, Egypt, Greece, and Germany. While in Kaiserswerth, Germany she heard about a Lutheran institution which trained young, middle class ladies to be nurses. It seemed like a sign to her.

FLORENCE GOES TO SCHOOL

Florence had already turned down several marriage proposals, and when she got back from Germany, she firmly announced that she would not marry. She would devote her life to caring for the sick.

Her parents finally accepted their daughter's wishes, and Florence went back to Kaiserswerth. This time as a student. During the three-month training course, she learned about the importance of cleanliness, nutrition, and fresh air in maintaining health. She also learned to make beds, bathe patients, and she even got to observe surgeries. She must have thought she was in heaven!

At age thirty-one, Florence finally achieved her lifelong dream of becoming a nurse. After graduating from the nursing course, she returned to England and got her first nursing job: She was in charge of organizing a Hospital for Gentlewomen on Harley Street in London.

CRIMEAN WAR

A few years later, the Crimean War broke out between Turkey and Russia, and in 1854 Great Britain joined alongside Turkey. They sent 30,000 British soldiers, a few doctors, a bit of medicine, and no nurses.

Then Florence received a letter from the General Secretary of State for War, Sidney Herbert. She had met him when she was visiting hospitals around Europe. He knew she had become a nurse, and he asked her to recruit a team of nurses for the Scutari hospital for wounded soldiers in Istanbul. Florence started interviewing. She talked to two hundred women and found only thirty-eight who she deemed suitable—most of them were nuns, who she knew would follow her instructions. Then Florence and her team set off for Turkey.

SCUTARI HOSPITAL

When they walked into the hospital, the ladies were horrified by the conditions. It was dark and smelly, very smelly. There were no beds and wounded men were lying on the floor with rats running around them. The patients were being fed stale and moldy food, and the toilet, which was no more than a hole in the floor, was overflowing. It's not surprising that some of the doctors thought this was no place for women.

Undaunted, Florence and her team went to work. They opened windows to let in fresh air, then they swept, mopped, and scrubbed everything. They bought beds, repaired pillows and blankets, had the toilets cleared, and got rid of the vermin. They began to serve the men healthy food, change their soiled bandages, and bathe them. The men's health improved, and doctors decided that nurses might just be useful after all.

LADY WITH THE LAMP

Florence believed that no man should die alone. So every night, after the other doctors and nurses had gone to bed, she would take her lamp and walk along the lines of beds which stretched for miles. She checked on each and every soldier. Florence became known as "The Lady with the Lamp" and was such a comfort to the injured men that some of them even kissed her shadow as she passed.

In 1856 after the war was over, Florence was preparing to return to England. She was surprised to learn that she had gained a bit of fame back home. The press had been reporting on her activities and the difference she had made in the care of the wounded. But Florence was just fulfilling her calling and wasn't looking for fanfare, so she traveled back home under an alias to avoid any attention.

LADY WITH THE PIE CHART

Unfortunately, Florence never fully recovered from a case of Crimean Fever which she contracted while overseas. By age thirty-eight, she was often bedridden and barely left her house. Even though she was in poor health the rest of her days, she didn't let that stop her. She just set down her lamp and took up drawing pie charts.

Florence wrote more than two hundred books and pamphlets expounding the benefits of a healthy diet, cleanliness, and fresh air in preventing disease. And she put her love of mathematics to good use by making infographics to show her data.

She used a sort of pie chart, which she called a coxcomb, to illustrate the number of deaths, and more importantly, causes of death in the military hospital. It clearly showed that many more soldiers died from preventable disease than from battle wounds. Her presentation convinced the government that health standards in military hospitals (and then all hospitals) needed to be upgraded.

NURSING SCHOOL

Florence had shown everyone what a difference trained and dedicated nurses could make. In 1860 she started her own nursing school at St. Thomas' Hospital in London. It was funded with donations from the public and was the first secular nursing school in the world. It's still in operation today as part of Kings College, London. Thanks to her, nursing became a respectable occupation.

Florence died in her sleep in 1910 at age ninety in her London home where she had lived since returning from the war. She was buried in a quiet ceremony near her childhood home, but there was also a public service held at St. Paul's Cathedral. It was attended by royalty and other important people. But Florence would have been most proud of the hundreds of young women who came to honor the lady who had inspired them to don their nurses' caps.

* The Florence Nightingale Museum is located at parking level on the grounds of St. Thomas' Hospital, 2 Lambeth Palace Road, London, SE1 7EW. It's the same location where Florence began her school in 1860.
* International Nurses Day is celebrated on 12 May, Florence Nightingale's birthday.

CALENDAR YEARS AND TAX YEARS
BRITS MUST PAY UP

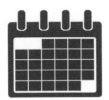

$\mathcal{C}$oming from America, I was used to the calendar year and tax year being the same: January 1 through December 31. So, I was surprised to find out that England's tax year was April 6 through April 5. How in the world did they arrive at these dates?

It seems the mystery lies in changing calendars and the government's determination to not miss one day of tax collecting. Let's have a look at the calendar situation first...

JULIAN CALENDAR

In 46 BC Julius Caesar gathered together his best astronomers and mathematicians in Rome to design a new calendar. He modestly called it the Julian calendar after himself. It set out the first day of the year as January 1.

But that didn't necessarily mean everyone accepted it as the first day of the year. Different countries and even different regions of countries celebrated the beginning of the year on various dates, with two common dates being March 25 and December 25.

But the Julian calendar did a pretty good job of keeping track of all the days and months. There was a tiny miscalculation of eleven minutes per year, but what could that hurt? Eleven minutes isn't much, it just added one extra day every 128 years. However, after a thousand years or so, the months were drifting into the wrong seasons.

GREGORIAN CALENDAR

So in 1582 the Vatican stepped in to sort things out. They came up with a new calendar, called the Gregorian Calendar, after Pope Gregory XIII. It kept New Year's Day as January 1 and put everything back in order. This new calendar was adopted by most of Europe, which was under the Pope's authority.

ENGLAND'S HAVING NONE OF IT

However, nearly 50 years earlier, King Henry VIII of England had thumbed his nose at the Pope and declared himself no longer under his control. So his Protestant daughter, now Queen Elizabeth I, wasn't about to let Rome tell her what day it was. She was having none of this newfangled calendar.

So, in an early version of Brexit, Britain carried on with its old calendar for 170 years, getting further and further out of sync with the rest of Europe. Businesspeople who traded with others around the globe had to use both dates to avoid confusion.

By 1752 the British calendar was eleven days off. It was time for Britain to swallow its pride and conform. It adopted the Gregorian calendar in September 1752. But what to do with those extra eleven days?

MISSING ELEVEN DAYS

They decided to just skip those pesky, surplus days. So everyone went to sleep on September 2, 1752 and woke up the next morning to September 14. To some people this was very disconcerting, and they feared that they might be losing eleven days of their lives.

However, at least one man saw an opportunity to make some money out of these missing days. He bet anyone who would take the bait that he could dance nonstop for 12 days. Of course, that seemed impossible and he had a few takers. He waited until the evening of September 2. He began his little jig and danced all night long. When he stopped the next day, it was September 14 and he collected his money on a technicality.

BRITS STILL HAVE TO PAY THEIR TAXES

So what does all this have to do with the UK tax year, and why does it begin on April 6?

Under the old Julian calendar, the British civil year and tax year both began on March 25. When the country changed to the new Gregorian calendar, January 1 became the first day of the civil year. The government didn't mind changing their civil year or losing eleven calendar days off their calendar. However, they drew the line at the thought of losing any tax collecting days.

So the Lords Commissioners of the Treasury decided not to align the tax year with the civil year. The old tax year began on March 25, so they just pushed it forward by eleven days to get their full 365 days' worth of taxes. This made the new tax year begin on April 5.

April 5 remained the first day of the British tax year until 1800, which would have been a leap year under the old calendar but wasn't one under the new one. Again, the Treasury wasn't about to lose out on one day of tax collecting, so they moved the tax year forward by one day, and this is where it has remained. Finally, the mystery of the April 6 to April 5 tax year is solved.

ST. GEORGE

ENGLISH DRAGON SLAYER
AND PATRON SAINT

$\mathcal{S}$t. George is the patron saint of England. His banner, bearing a red cross on a white background, adorns England's flag and waves at every football match. George is often represented as an English knight gallantly fighting a dragon and rescuing a princess. But who was the real George? Was he English? And did he really fight dragons?

GEORGE THE ROMAN SOLDIER

St. George is based on a real person, but his story is a murky mixture of fact and fiction. We know he was born in the third century in Cappadocia, Turkey, to Greek Christian parents, and we know he became a soldier in the Roman army.

Around the year 300 AD, the Roman Emperor Diocletian began a campaign of persecution against Christians. And he started with the Christians in the Roman army. All Roman soldiers were forced to show their loyalty by making a sacrifice to the Roman gods. If they refused, they would be kicked out of the army, punished, or even executed.

GEORGE THE MARTYR

Of course, George, being a good Christian, refused to bow to the Roman gods. Legend says he was jailed—and this is where the fiction possibly kicks in—and tortured for seven years. He was beaten, boiled in hot oil, forced to drink poison, had spikes run through him, etc. It seems that none of this had any effect on George—he didn't even have a headache.

George's endurance of all these tortures drew even more people to Christianity, which really upset the Romans. Finally, on 23 April 303, George was beheaded, and that was the end of George… but not the end of his story. He lived on as a popular warrior saint.

GEORGE THE MEDIEVAL KNIGHT

Now, let's skip ahead about ten centuries, to Europe in the era of the Crusades. Countless knights clad in chain mail armor are steering their gallant steeds toward the Holy Land. There they hear stories about George, the warrior saint, and he becomes their hero.

Although the real George never set foot on English shores, the returning knights brought his story with them. And George is transformed. No longer is he a Roman soldier—he becomes a medieval English knight. And, like all great knights worth their salt, he rescues a princess and slays a fearsome dragon—in Oxfordshire, England.

THE LEGEND

Printed versions of George's heroic deeds pop up around the 12th century and they go something like this...

A certain kingdom had a dragon problem. To keep the hungry dragon satisfied, the people were feeding him two sheep per day. They would tie them out on the hill near the river where the monster lived and he would come along and gobble them up.

But the people couldn't raise sheep fast enough, and soon they had to leave one sheep and one person for the dragon. Since not many people volunteered to be dragon dinner, a lottery was started. The King thought his family should be exempt, but his subjects had other ideas. It was his sweet daughter who convinced the King that they were all in this together and they all had to take their chances with the lottery.

Sure enough, a few weeks later, the Princess' name was drawn. The King was heartbroken and begged for someone to take her place. Even though the people felt sad for their Princess, no one was keen to be eaten.

The brave Princess prepared herself for her fate. She put on her best gown and tied ribbons in her hair. Then she was led out to the hill and tied to a stake along with a sheep. There she awaited her certain death.

GEORGE THE DRAGON SLAYER

Then George in his shining armor rode up on a white steed. He stopped in front of the tearful Princess. "Why are you crying, My Lady? And why are you tied to a post with a sheep?"

"You better get out of here," she sobbed, "or you'll end up as dragon food too."

But chivalrous knight that George was, he could never leave a damsel in distress. He stayed and listened to her tale about the dragon whose dinner she was meant to be. While they were talking, the ground began to shake. The dragon was on his way—running toward them. The beast was drooling with excitement because he thought he was having knight and horse for dessert.

George jumped on his steed and pulled out his lance. Then he made the sign of the cross and galloped toward the monster. As they collided, George's spear ran right through the dragon who fell to the ground moaning. George untied the Princess and told her to take off her belt and tie it around the dragon's neck. Then they led the dragon back to the city like a little dog on a leash.

When the people saw the dragon, they were afraid. They ran into their houses and peeked out the windows. George said, "Don't be afraid. Believe in God and be baptized, and I will slay this dragon." So the King and all the people ran to the pond where George baptized them all. Then George cut off the dragon's head and peace returned to the kingdom.

Everyone was grateful to George, and the King offered him a pile of riches. But the gallant knight refused, telling him to give it to the poor. The King promised to build churches and be a good Christian, and George rode off into the sunset.

GEORGE THE PATRON SAINT

The medieval knights were so inspired by St. George's story, that they adopted him as their protective saint. When they rode into battle, they carried his banner: A red cross on a white background. St. George officially became English when King Edward III made him the patron saint of England around 1350.

His exploits were transferred to England too. The place where he had performed his knightly feats became associated with Oxfordshire. A hill near Uffington is said to be the place where the damsel was offered, and the dragon slain. As proof, there's a chalk-white spot at the top where nothing will grow. Obviously it's because that's where the dragon's blood seeped into the earth and poisoned it.

George isn't just an English saint. Knights from all over Europe came back from the Crusades singing his praises, and he's patron saint of several countries, areas, and cities, including Catalonia. There, on St. George's day women are presented with roses and men are given books. It seems that everyone loves a good knight's tale.

* Dragon hill is located in the town of Uffington in the county of Oxfordshire. It's about two hours from London, or one hour from Oxford, or a bit over an hour from Bath.
* Just next to Dragon Hill you will find the Uffington White Horse which is a Bronze age chalk carving.

VII

NAPOLEON BONAPARTE

THE MAN THE ENGLISH LOVE TO HATE

It might seem odd to talk about a French emperor in a book about England. But there was a time when the very mention of Napoleon Bonaparte's name set the British people shaking in their boots.

They were terrified that he would invade their shores at any moment, and they used the threat of him to scare children into behaving. But most of all, they really liked to make fun of him.

BONEY THE BOGEYMAN

NAPOLEON SCARES BRITISH CHILDREN

*I*n the early 1800s Napoleon Bonaparte was skipping across Europe gathering up countries as if they were flowers. He was keen to add Britain to his bouquet, and the British knew it. In an effort to belittle the emperor and play down the threat he posed, the Brits gave him the nickname "Little Boney." Their propaganda showed "Little Boney" as a tiny man across from a meaty "John Bull" (the personification of England).

FROM LITTLE BONEY TO BONEY THE BOGEYMAN

Even though "Little Boney" was miniaturized in the media, when British parents told their children about him, he was larger than life. He became "Boney the Bogeyman" and was used to frighten boys and girls into obedience: "If you don't behave, Boney will come for you!" Boney morphed into a giant ogre who would carry off misbehaving children and eat them for breakfast.

One British humorist, G.A. a'Beckett, wrote about his childhood during those years and his boyish impressions of Boney. He was attending a preparatory school for "young gentlemen from three to eight" near Kensington in southwest London. Below is a paraphrase of his memories:

It was 1815 and Bonaparte had just escaped from Elba Island where he had been exiled. The teacher, Miss Frounce, took full advantage of the situation to strike fear into the hearts of her students and keep her classroom of "young gentlemen from three to eight" under control.

Bonaparte was presented as the "great bugbear" and every boy in the school was afraid of him. They knew that if they misbehaved or didn't learn their lessons properly, Miss Frounce would happily turn them over to Boney, that child-eating ogre. And they were certain that if Boney landed on British shores he would head straight for their school. He would knock at the door, then Miss Frounce would gladly hand over the misbehaving boys to him.

One day it was announced that a leg of mutton was missing from the school larder, and panic set in among the boys. They had no doubt about the identity of the thief. It could be none other than Boney. He must have landed during the night and stolen their provisions. Secretly they were relieved it was a leg of mutton that had been his dinner and not one of them. Miss Frounce didn't contradict the boys. She thought it proved her point that Boney was near and the boys had better behave.

BONEY THE MAN

Later, in 1815, when Napoleon was exiled on St Helena, another British child had a chance to meet Boney in person. Betsy Balcombe lived in St Helena with her family and the Emperor stayed in their guesthouse while his own home was being built.

Betsy had grown up hearing all the fearful tales about Boney. But now, at the ripe old age of fourteen, she no longer believed that he was a fire-breathing, child-eating ogre. Still, she was very nervous and frightened when she heard that he would be coming, not only to the island where she lived, but to her home. She was the only one in her family who spoke French well, so the job of interpreter fell to her. To her surprise, she found Boney to be charming and decidedly un-ogreish. They became great friends and often teased one another—both having a mischievous side.

Once a British woman visited the house with her young daughter. Like other British children, she had been warned many times about Boney snatching away naughty children. So, she was terrified to hear that Boney lived there.

Betsy went to the Emperor and told him the girl was afraid of him, then she brought him into the room. Being in a playful mood, Napoleon pulled back his hair, made faces and howled. The poor little girl went into a panic. She had to be carried from the room and it took some time for her mother to calm her. Meanwhile, Boney was bewildered to learn of his child-eating reputation and that the very mention of his name was enough to make British children stop fighting, sit up straight, or do their school lessons. He hadn't realized he was quite that powerful!

When his house was complete, Betsy was sad to see Napoleon go. Since her father was Napoleon's purveyor, he visited weekly and Betsy went along as often as she could. They continued their close friendship until Betsy's family left the island.

She later wrote about her experience with Napoleon in a book, *Recollections of the Emperor Napoleon: During the first three years of his captivity on the island of St. Helena.*

In the end, Boney never actually made it to England and no British children were eaten. However, that didn't stop the threats. Even into the twentieth century, one could occasionally hear a grandmother warn a misbehaving child that if they didn't straighten up Boney would come get them.

WHO HUNG THE MONKEY?
AND WAS HE REALLY A FRENCH SPY?

*a*bout 200 years ago, the people of Hartlepool hung a monkey who was accused of being one of Napoleon's spies.

THE LEGEND GOES LIKE THIS...

It was in the early 1800s in the small town of Hartlepool on the coast of northeast England. The local fishermen were out in their boats when they caught sight of a French ship. The Napoleonic Wars were still raging after many years and had cost the lives of thousands of men. So when the Hartlepudlians (that's what they call people from Hartlepool) saw that the French ship was having trouble and sinking, they weren't too unhappy about it. And they sure didn't row out to try and save the men aboard.

They headed back to the safety of their own land and set up watch to make sure that none of those Frenchies swam to their shores. While they waited, they had a few drinks (or maybe more) and talked about what they would do if a Frenchman dared to appear on their beach. They would question him and get all the information they could about Napoleon and what his next move might be. They might even gain information that could put an end to the war and make Hartlepool famous at the same time.

Then they caught a glimpse of a survivor. He was clinging to a piece of the broken ship, and the sea was carrying him directly toward the fishermen. They ran out and surrounded the unfortunate chap. They grabbed his arms (which they noticed were extremely long and hairy) and tied them behind his back. He was an odd looking fellow: He was very short, and it wasn't only his arms that were hairy—he was very hairy all over.

As it turned out, this hairy little man was a monkey: The ship's mascot dressed in a little French military uniform. (It's more likely that he was a chimp since there's no mention of a tail, and monkeys have tails. Chimps and Frenchmen do not.) The Hartlepudlians had never seen a monkey. They had never seen a Frenchman either, for that matter. However, they had seen British cartoons depicting Napoleon as being very short so they weren't surprised that this French sailor was also on the short side. And as for all that hair? Well, some men are hairier than others—no real cause for concern.

They took the monkey to the town square and began to question him. In answer to every question, he just screeched and chattered in a language they didn't understand. They could only assume it was French. He simply refused to speak English which infuriated the Hartlepool folk even more since they knew that everyone could speak English if they wanted to.

After questioning the poor monkey for hours and failing to get any answers in their native tongue, they held a trial and convicted him of being a French spy. He was sentenced to die by hanging. A gallows was made from bits of the shipwreck, and the poor little monkey was hanged in the town square.

Well, that's the legend anyway and it's an important part of Hartlepool's folklore.

FROM INSULT TO SOURCE OF PRIDE

"Who hung the monkey?" became a way to insult the people of Old Hartlepool. In the mid 1800s, there were two Hartlepools: Old and West. West Hartlepool was the newer, more modern town. Those from this new town looked at Old Hartlepudlians as being ignorant and behind the times.

So whenever insults were being thrown around between the two, invariably the West Hartlepool side would come out with, "Oh yeah? Well, who hung the monkey?" It was an insult: How could they be so daft as to confuse a monkey with a Frenchman? Eventually, however, the two sides grew together to form a single Hartlepool, and the monkey legend became a source of city pride.

In 1999 the Hartlepool United Football Club took a monkey as their mascot. His name is H'Angus (note the word "hang" in his name). One of the men who wore the mascot costume even ran for mayor (wearing the monkey suit) and campaigned on the promise of "free bananas for all schoolchildren." And he won, by the way. In fact, he was elected mayor in 2002, 2005, and 2009.

ANOTHER MONKEY TALE

A similar Napoleonic monkey story is told a bit further up the coast in Boddam, Scotland, a fishing village near Aberdeen. As in the first version, this one has a French shipwreck and a surviving monkey who is hanged. However, the Boddam fishermen had a different motive. They claim that they knew the monkey wasn't a French spy. But they also knew that "finders keepers" was the law for shipwrecks, so they would be entitled to whatever treasures might be on board the doomed ship—but only if there were no survivors. Would a monkey count as a survivor? They didn't want to take that chance, so they hung the monkey.

IS IT TRUE?

Could the strange story of a monkey being hung as a French spy be true? It seems that the first mention of this monkey tale is from around 1854 when the Victorian entertainer, Ned Corvan, wrote a song about it which he performed in Hartlepool. Other than that, there's no historical record to support that it actually happened.

The Hartlepudlians got a bit excited in 2005 when a strange bone washed up on their shores. For a while everyone thought it was a monkey bone and that their city's legend might be proven once and for all. But, disappointingly, it turned out to be a fossilized prehistoric deer bone. So we still don't know if the hairy little fellow in the French uniform was actually hanged.

WHEN NAPOLEON
MET HIS BUNNYLOO

RABBITS PUT THE EMPEROR TO FLIGHT

*E*ngland and France have a long history of fighting each other (once they did so for 100 years). Now, even though they're no longer enemies, they still like to have a laugh at one another's expense. So, the Brits that got wind of this story in the early 1800s must have loved it...

It seems that several years before Napoleon's ill-fated battle at Waterloo, he suffered another humiliating defeat. This time at the hands (or paws) of furry little bunny rabbits.

Louis-Alexandre Berthier (let's just call him Berti) was Napoleon's Chief of Staff and Minister of War. He was in charge of the army, and it was said of him, that "no one could have better suited General Bonaparte, who wanted a man capable of relieving him of all detailed work, to understand him instantly and to foresee what he would need."

BERTI'S BLUNDER

But there was one unfortunate instance where Berti's attention to detail let him (and his Emperor) down. It was late summer 1806 and the hunting season had just begun. Berti wanted to host an event to impress and entertain his Emperor, so he organized a rabbit hunt. He owned a piece of land outside Paris that was just perfect. Except for one minor detail... there were no rabbits on the land.

But Berti didn't let the lack of rabbits worry him—rabbits could be bought easily enough. He had organized so many complicated military matters for the Emperor, that a little rabbit hunt would be a doddle. So, he sent out his servant to buy 1,000 rabbits—that should be more than enough to make sure everyone could get a few and ensure the Emperor a jolly good time.

However, Berti didn't specify which kind of rabbits the servant should buy. Perhaps he (like the servant) assumed that all bunnies would be the same. Surely tame rabbits that had been raised in hutches would be just as much fun to hunt as their wild cousins—and they were easier to obtain.

The morning of the hunt rolled around and Berti checked his list. All was going to schedule. Breakfast was being cooked and the rabbits were in the field. Everything was ready for the Emperor. At the appointed hour, Napoleon's carriage rolled up. He was accompanied by high-ranking military officers and other important men, and they were all looking forward to a good day of sport.

THE RABBIT HUNT

After a hearty breakfast, they headed out for the hunt. The 1,000 tame rabbits had been turned loose in the field, but those poor bunnies had never been alone in a big, open field. They didn't know what to do, so they huddled together in one large mass. And when they saw the hunters arrive, instead of fleeing in fear, as wild rabbits would have, they were happy to see humans. They could only assume they were coming to feed them, as they hadn't yet had breakfast and their tummies were rumbling.

The bunnies bounded in one large furry mob toward a surprised Emperor Napoleon and his band of hunters. At first the men were shocked and amused. They had never seen rabbits act like this—no one had. But the laughter subsided as the throng of rabbits drew closer and showed no signs of stopping. One little rabbit would be nothing to fear, but 1,000 hungry, bouncing bunnies was a different story. The men started to hit at them with their rifles and sticks, but they just kept hopping all around them.

WHO'S HUNTING WHOM?

Berti, who was horrified at the turn of events, took control with military precision. He called for the coachmen to bring their whips to drive away the scary bunnies. The whips did frighten the rabbits and they turned around and fled. The hunters laughed again at this strange occurrence and thought it was just a humorous little delay to the start of their hunt.

The rabbits, who seemed to have tactical manoeuvers of their own, split into two sections, one went to the right and the other to the left. The hunters were collecting themselves and Berti was apologizing profusely for this strange occurrence, when suddenly they were attacked from behind. The rabbits had just circled around and come back after Napoleon.

The little guy in the big hat looked like he was in charge, so he probably had the food. And the hungry bunnies weren't leaving until they had had their breakfast. They were bouncing in famished impatience all around Napoleon. Everyone tried to beat them away. But they were so eager to find their food that they were hopping up on top of each other and were halfway up Napoleon's legs so that he could only stagger as he tried to escape toward his carriage.

The mighty Napoleon and his men were forced to retreat. The Emperor was exhausted when he finally reached the safety of his carriage. Even there, a few bunnies had managed to enter by hopping onto the heads of the others. Apparently, they were looking for a ride back to their nice safe hutch and a quiet lunch. Instead, they were unceremoniously thrown out the carriage window as the Emperor was hurried away from the battlefield.

Everyone met back at Berti's place to have a good stout drink to recover from their ordeal and to talk about their bizarre experience. No one had ever seen rabbits behave like that. Were the animals mad? Possessed by some evil magic? No one could come up with an explanation.

Berti was horrified that his carefully plotted event had gone so wrong. He called the servant in charge of procuring rabbits, who admitted that his knowledge of rabbits was limited, and he had thought one rabbit was as good as another. Therefore, he had purchased rabbits that had been raised in a hutch. This explained why they looked at humans as their source of food instead of a source of danger.

DON'T TELL

Berti was embarrassed, and the other fellows had a good laugh at his expense. However, they didn't really want word to get out that the great Napoleon, who had been defeating armies all over Europe, had been forced to retreat by a bunch of bunnies. So, they all pinky-swore never to speak of it again.

But somehow Baron Thiébault got word of it. He didn't like Berti, so he relished the tale of his bunny blunder and wrote it down in his memoirs so everyone could have a laugh at him and his Emperor running from the rabbits. However, it didn't go to print until after all those involved were long gone.

I can't help but wonder... when Napoleon was at that fateful Battle of Waterloo and it all started to go wrong for him, did his mind go back to his earlier defeat at the Battle of Bunnyloo?

- This story is adapted from *The memoirs of Baron Thiébault (late lieutenant-general in the French army)* Translated and condensed by Arthur John Butler - Publication date 1896.

LIKE WHAT YOU'VE READ?

LEAVE A REVIEW AND TELL OTHERS

I hope you've enjoyed this collection of Curious Histories of England. If you have, I would really appreciate it if you would leave a review on Amazon, Goodreads, or whichever bookstore you bought it through.

And don't forget to recommend it to your friends. Spread the word and spread the cheer!

Thank you in advance.

ABOUT MARGO

HELLO, LET ME INTRODUCE MYSELF

I'm American by birth but feel at home in Europe after years of living in the UK and France. Life is never dull here with so much history to discover. It seems there are stories hiding around every corner and buried under every flagstone. So I'm always peeking around pillars and pulling up pavement to find them.

I'm curious by nature, and I'm forever wanting to know who, what, why, when, where, and how... When I find answers to my many questions, I share them on my blog, the *Curious Rambler*, and in my *Curious Histories* books—like this one. (Are you beginning to notice a "curious" theme here?)

I share my adventures (and my multitude of questions) with Jeff, my husband of many years. I enjoy travel, history, observing cultures and traditions—and then writing about them, of course.

You can follow me on my website: *CuriousRambler.com*.

Thank you for reading.

OTHER BOOKS BY MARGO

LOOKING FOR SOMETHING ELSE TO READ?

BERETS, BAGUETTES, AND BEYOND:
Curious Histories of France
— If you love all things French, you'll be intrigued by the
stories behind everyday French items such as the beret and
striped shirts. Find out why a rooster represents France, how
baguettes got their shape, and much more...

FRENCH HOLIDAYS & TRADITIONS
— Delve into the curious traditions the French celebrate
throughout the year. You'll discover what fish have to do with
the first of April, why the French hand out poisonous
flowers on the first day of May, what mice have to do with
children's teeth, and more...

CURIOUS HISTORIES OF NICE, FRANCE

— Uncover intriguing tales of the people and events that shaped this city on the French Riviera. Read about Queen Victoria riding around Nice in a donkey cart, how the local specialty may have started out as ammunition, why a cannon announces lunch time, and much more...

A TASTE OF NICE, FRANCE

This free e-book complements Curious Histories of Nice, France and contains even more stories about Nice and the surrounding area.

CURIOUS HISTORIES OF PROVENCE:
Tales from the South of France

— Discover the legends and histories of that magical place in the south of France called Provence. Learn why the cicadas sing so loudly, what happened to the local dragon, how Buffalo Bill influenced the area, and more...

ANIMAL TALES: Ten Modern Fables

— Through these ten charming animal stories, children will enjoy learning that everyone is different and that these differences don't make them better or worse than anyone else. Each fable is followed by a short moral take-away. It's an engaging and fun way to help children embrace diversity.

Printed in Great Britain
by Amazon